History of Peru

A Captivating Guide to Peruvian History, Starting from the Chavín Civilization and Other Ancient Andean Civilizations through the Inca Empire to the Present

© Copyright 2023 - All rights reserved.

The content contained within this book may not be reproduced, duplicated, or transmitted without direct written permission from the author or the publisher.

Under no circumstances will any blame or legal responsibility be held against the publisher, or author, for any damages, reparation, or monetary loss due to the information contained within this book, either directly or indirectly.

Legal Notice:

This book is copyright protected. It is only for personal use. You cannot amend, distribute, sell, use, quote, or paraphrase any part, or the content within this book, without the consent of the author or publisher.

Disclaimer Notice:

Please note the information contained within this document is for educational and entertainment purposes only. All effort has been executed to present accurate, up-to-date, reliable, and complete information. No warranties of any kind are declared or implied. Readers acknowledge that the author is not engaging in the rendering of legal, financial, medical, or professional advice. The content within this book has been derived from various sources. Please consult a licensed professional before attempting any techniques outlined in this book.

By reading this document, the reader agrees that under no circumstances is the author responsible for any losses, direct or indirect, that are incurred as a result of the use of the information contained within this document, including, but not limited to, errors, omissions, or inaccuracies.

Free Bonus from Captivating History (Available for a Limited time)

Hi History Lovers!

Now you have a chance to join our exclusive history list so you can get your first history ebook for free as well as discounts and a potential to get more history books for free! Simply visit the link below to join.

Captivatinghistory.com/ebook

Also, make sure to follow us on Facebook, Twitter and Youtube by searching for Captivating History.

Table of Contents

INTRODUCTION: A NATION STEEPED IN HISTORY 1
CHAPTER 1 - THE RISE OF THE INCA EMPIRE 4
CHAPTER 2 - THE FIRST PHASE OF THE SPANISH CONQUEST 12
CHAPTER 3 - THE LAST DAYS OF THE INCAN EMPIRE 29
CHAPTER 4 - LAST GASPS OF REBELLION 39
CHAPTER 5 - POST-INCA LIFE IN PERU 46
CHAPTER 6 - PERUVIAN INDEPENDENCE 55
CHAPTER 7 - THE WAR OF THE PACIFIC AND THE MODERNIZATION OF PERU 62
CHAPTER 8 - THE DAWNING OF A NEW CENTURY 68
CHAPTER 9 - FROM MILITARY DICTATORSHIP TO MODERN PERU 74
CHAPTER 10 - PERU TODAY—A PRECARIOUS STATE? 81
CONCLUSION: BRIGHTER DAYS AHEAD 85
HERE'S ANOTHER BOOK BY CAPTIVATING HISTORY THAT YOU MIGHT LIKE 87
FREE BONUS FROM CAPTIVATING HISTORY (AVAILABLE FOR A LIMITED TIME) 88
APPENDIX A: FURTHER READING AND REFERENCE 89

Introduction: A Nation Steeped in History

Many may not be aware of the details of the long and continuous history of Peruvian civilization, but it is safe to say the depth of Peruvian culture is stunning. And it is right to say that the history of Peru is the history of the continuation of an ancient civilization. Even though the Inca giants were toppled by the Spaniards, the Peruvian civilization and culture of which they were a part were not snuffed out.

Although it is true that Peruvians learned Spanish, largely converted to Catholicism, and learned to adapt in many ways, the core structure of the original Peruvian culture is still largely intact. The settlement of what is today Peru is believed to have begun some twenty thousand years ago. It is thought the Peruvians got their start from the great migration that occurred during the last ice age when an ice bridge allowed people to cross the Bering Strait.

The people who would one day inhabit Peru made their way down the western coasts of the Americas until they settled into the mountainous lands of what we now know as Peru. Ancient tools and weapons have been discovered in Peru that date back well over ten thousand years ago. These ancient peoples were largely hunters and gatherers who followed the food that they ate as they roamed the rugged landscape.

This nomadic lifestyle began to shift toward a rooted agricultural one once the highly suitable farming lands of the Huaca Prieta and Kotosh regions were discovered. The soil is rich there, and even a novice farmer would not have too hard of a time growing some good crops. So, it makes sense that at this point in time, many farming implements emerged in the archaeological record.

There is also evidence that the domestication of animals became quite common at this point in Peruvian history. A further indication of settled society can be found in artifacts like knitted wool, woven baskets, and carefully crafted clay pottery. These are all signs of a settled society, and they can be found dating back thousands of years before Columbus ever set sail to the New World.

The Peruvians established the first major settlements in the Andes region in a place known as Caral. This settlement was situated some 125 miles from the modern-day city of Lima. This city is said to have been over one hundred acres and was likely home to thousands of inhabitants. As the town progressed, the architecture of the settlement became more impressive. Eventually, the town even boasted ancient pyramid-type structures.

The city would be the home of an ancient tribe of Peruvians who would later be known as the Norte Chico, which is Spanish for "Little North." The Norte Chico were just one group that came to dominance in the Peruvian landscape. Due to migration, natural disasters, and civil unrest, the population would ebb and flow.

On the heels of the Norte Chico group was the Chavín civilization, which would come to prominence around 1000 BCE. The Chavín civilization was centered around the Andes in the Mosna Valley. Many archaeologists believe the settlement likely began as a ceremonial worship center with pyramid-shaped temples situated in a plaza before dwellings developed around this sacred place of worship.

Like many then and now, the Chavín seemed to have placed much value on their own sense of spirituality. This is evidenced by the fact that a sacred site of worship would quite literally be the centerpiece of their lives. The great care taken for this place of worship is indicated by the lengths that were taken to preserve it from the elements. Since the Andean Highlands often flood, canals were created to serve as a drainage system to keep the temple from sustaining water damage.

The dwellings that spiraled out from the Chavín worship site continued to grow until the settlement boasted a population of roughly three thousand. Even though the settlement likely initially centered around the religious aspects of the Chavín, it was not long before settlers and religious pilgrims began to trade with each other. According to the archaeological record, there was a robust trade of in-demand goods, such as squash, beans, corn, and alpaca wool.

The Chavín were also skilled artisans and are notable for boasting some of the earliest artworks in the region. Chavín pottery and sculptures show an attention to detail and an imaginative streak. Some works of art seem to be taken directly from the world around them, while others depict mythical beasts and even anthropomorphized creatures, such as figures with a mixture of human and reptilian features.

The Chavín civilization was a robust one and has been categorized by archaeologists as having three distinct phases. There was the Urabarriu stage, which ran from roughly 900 to 500 BCE and consisted of just a couple of settlements anchored by the Chavín religious center. Then there was the Chakinani phase, which lasted from 500 to 400 BCE, by which time the settlements had completely encircled the religious shrines. This was then followed by the Jarabarriu stage, which lasted from 400 to 250 BCE. During this final stage, the Chavín civilization experienced a population boom, and the settlement went from loosely connected villages to a dense center of development. Its influence quickly spread to surrounding regions.

Many more Andean civilizations would spring from the Chavín civilization. Ultimately, there would be a multitude of diverse people groups in that part of South America—that is, until one group rose above them all. And that group was the Incas.

Chapter 1 – The Rise of the Inca Empire

"America did not need to be discovered because quite simply America had the American-Indians. There were whole groups of people that already lived there including very developed societies such as the Incas, the Aztecs, and the Mayans. But then came the European vision that saw the conquest as a source of advanced growth away from medieval Europe. The new revolutionary bourgeois trend formed a new perspective on what was democracy that they saw as an improvement to the democracy of ancient Greece."

-Alejandro Castro Espín

The Inca Empire is, without a doubt, one of the most powerful civilizations ever to emerge in the pre-Columbian Americas. The Incas reigned supreme from 1438 to 1533 CE. The Inca Empire stretched across much of southwestern South America. The lands that the Incas came to dominate included modern-day Peru, much of Argentina, western Bolivia, southwestern Ecuador, and a chunk of Chile.

Prior to the rise of the Incas, there were a couple of important civilizations in the region. Before the Inca, there were the Tiwanaku, whose civilization lasted from 300 to 1000 CE, and the Wari, which spanned from 500 to 1000 CE. The Tiwanaku were based out of what today makes up a large section of western Bolivia.

Although this civilization collapsed, the influence that it created in this part of the world is still evident among the people of both Peru and

Bolivia. The Tiwanaku were an agricultural-based society centered around farming. They were also noted as being a multicultural society, which means many different tribes came together to forge a solid social compact.

The solidarity of these ancient tribes was centered around not only food but also religion. Several great monuments were constructed, attracting people from all over the region. It is believed that people regularly traveled several miles just to see some of the religious sites and pay homage to them. Evidence of these pilgrimages can be seen in the archaeological record by way of sacrificial offerings at altars, as well as through plenty of other artifacts that were left behind along the way.

The Tiwanaku was indeed a robust and vibrant civilization, so what happened to it? Although no one knows for sure, it has been suggested that the civilization faced some sort of environmental calamity, such as a very bad drought, which could have led to poor harvests and, ultimately, famine. Complex civilizations cannot survive without an abundance of food, so this would make for a likely explanation.

It has also been theorized that there was some sort of social breakdown that led to civil unrest. The upheaval had to have been bad enough to rend the very fabric of society. Lending credence to this theory is purported evidence that the capital had sustained major damage by force. It is believed gates were smashed and monuments were tipped over long ago by the inhabitants of this region. But why? Since there was no written record left behind, we can only wonder.

Even in the absence of the written word, there is an indication of a great migration of refugees from whatever crisis these people faced. There are signs that a major movement of people from this region headed south toward Chile at this time.

Nearly simultaneous to the establishment and growth of the Tiwanaku was the Wari people. As mentioned, the Wari had their heyday roughly from 500 to 1000 CE. Some have argued that perhaps the Wari is an offshoot of the Tiwanaku, but this still remains to be seen. At any rate, the Wari was a complex society in its own right, as indicated by the complex roadways that were established from various centers of trade under its dominion.

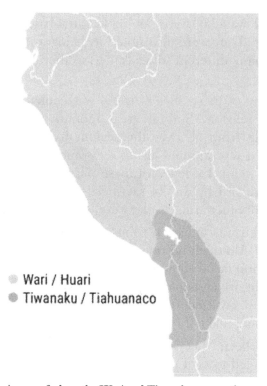

A map of where the Wari and Tiwanaku were active.
QQuantum, CC BY-SA 4.0 <https://creativecommons.org/licenses/by-sa/4.0>, via Wikimedia Commons https://commons.wikimedia.org/wiki/File:Map_of_Wari_and_Tiawaku.svg

The Wari not only grew food but also had active trading centers in which members of this society bartered for different items. Adding to the notion that the Wari was a complex civilization was the 2003 find of an elaborate royal tomb, which rivaled anything ever found in ancient Egypt. The tomb was like something found in one of Cairo's pyramids and had every indication of being the burial site of some very important personage. Archaeologists also found several servants in the tomb.

Nevertheless, their sudden disappearance from the archaeological record is just as perplexing as that of the Tiwanaku. The likely cause of the Wari's demise is a major drought. If it was indeed drought that contributed to the collapse of these two robust civilizations, it is theorized that the Incas' ability to rise above this particular challenge led to their own rise as a dominant civilization.

The Incas made themselves practically impervious to drought. They accomplished this with their masterful irrigation techniques. The Incas developed irrigation methods that allowed them to expertly run water from one location to another, carefully distributing this precious resource as needed, even during times of drought.

The Incas began as a small and obscure tribe among many and hailed from Cuzco (also spelled Cusco), Peru. The Incas likely raised cattle and herded their livestock in the plains. The Incas gifted us with a rich oral history, which allows them to tell some of their stories for themselves. Although rich in mythological musings, they do have their own ancestral origin story.

According to the traditional Inca narrative, three special caves were all lined up next to each other. The center cave was dubbed Quapaq T'uqu. Next to this cave were two others: Maras T'uqu and Sutiq T'uqu. Once upon a time, a group of people—four brothers and four sisters—emerged out of the center cave, Quapaq T'uqu. Leading the group was a man named Ayar Manco, who wielded a golden staff.

Supposedly, Manco would go around slamming this gold staff into the ground at various points before officially designating these locales as suitable places for his people to live. The other people in this origin story faced various trials and tribulations along the way.

According to Inca lore, the region of Cuzco eventually became the ideal spot for settlement. It is said that this was the final place Manco shoved his golden staff into the earth, indicating that the land was ripe for civilization. The great Manco would become known as Manco Cápac, and this "Inca Moses," who had led his people out of the wilderness, would become known as the founder of Inca society.

It has been said that the Kingdom of Cuzco was established under Manco. After Manco, the next great leader was said to be Pachacuti Yupanqui, who was hailed as Sapa Inca or "paramount leader." The Sapa Incas would be the central figures of the Inca Empire, as they wielded authority over all political, social, and military decisions.

The Sapa Inca was also in charge of constructing the great monuments and temples of the Inca civilization. These powerful leaders established great roads and, of course, impressive irrigation networks, which would be the lifeblood of the Inca Empire. The Sapa Inca was viewed as semi-divine and depicted on a golden throne with an elaborate crown or helmet on his head.

Sapa Inca Pachacuti Yupanqui began the so-called Inca age of expansion, which started in the year 1438. Under the leadership of Pachacuti Yupanqui, the Incas went from a small regional power to a great and sprawling empire. His name literally translates as "Earth Shaker," and it seems that he really did know how to shake things up.

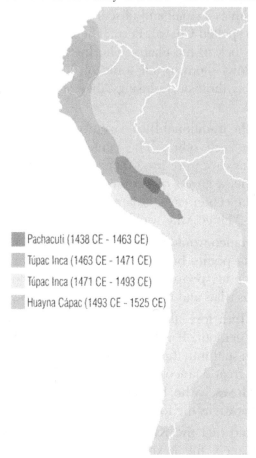

A look at Inca expansion.
QQuantum, CC BY-SA 4.0 <https://creativecommons.org/licenses/by-sa/4.0>, via Wikimedia Commons https://commons.wikimedia.org/wiki/File:Inca_Expansion.svg

The Incas became the dominant military power in the region. They used this dominance to subject the weaker tribes and make them pay allegiance to the Sapa Inca. Those who found themselves targeted by the Incas had limited options. They could fight (and most likely lose), flee, or join the Inca Empire. As much as the Spanish conquest would be criticized later on, the Incas were also living by the ancient rule of might makes right.

Today, in more civilized times, we can see the error in the stronger lording over the weaker, but during the rise of the Inca Empire, things were seen differently. As it pertained to those who were less adept at military prowess, they were either killed off, driven out, or incorporated into the growing tapestry of the Inca civilization.

Pachacuti Yupanqui, the ninth Sapa Inca, was just about as important as the founder and the first king. Under his rule, the greatest foe of the Incas (besides the Spanish, who came later), the Chimú, were defeated in battle. After the Chimú were put down, the Incas were able to expand into what is now known as southwestern South America.

Historians also believe that Machu Picchu was built, or at least began construction, during Pachacuti Yupanqui's reign. This majestic site in southern Peru was built on a mountain ridge that is around eight thousand feet. The Inca did not have a written language, although they did record important information with quipu, colored threads that were knotted in different ways to denote different numbers. Because of this, it is hard to know what Machu Picchu was used for, as it is believed the site was abandoned by the time the Spanish conquered the Incas. Most scholars believe it was either a place for royals to spend time or a sacred site for the Inca religion. Regardless of what it was used for, it draws hundreds of thousands of visitors every year today.

A view of Machu Picchu.
audrey_sel, CC BY-SA 2.0 <https://creativecommons.org/licenses/by-sa/2.0>, via Wikimedia Commons; https://commons.wikimedia.org/wiki/File:Sunset_across_Machu_Picchu.jpg

Inca society is fascinating. Many languages were spoken within the realm. They had a polytheistic religion and typically worshiped gods associated with nature. The Incas practiced human sacrifice, including child sacrifice, and the nobility also practiced cranial deformation. They would tie tight cloths around newborns' heads when their skulls were soft to create a more conical skull. The nobility would also be mummified upon death. The Inca buried their dead in the fetal position, which was supposed to imitate the womb and help those who died to be reborn in the next life.

Although Inca astronomers could not predict eclipses, they did know about solstices, equinoxes, and the zenith. They had two calendars, one based on the sun and one based on the moon, and they knew basic arithmetic, including the number zero.

The Inca Empire was governed in a rather predictable way, as its style of governance could be seen in many other parts of the world at different times and in different locales. Just like the Roman Empire of old, the Inca Empire consisted of a single centralized emperor (the Sapa Inca) who ruled over regional governors. There were four main provinces, which were led by the strongest regional leaders.

A map of the four provinces or suyus of the empire.
English Wikipedia user EuroHistoryTeacher, CC BY-SA 3.0
<*https://creativecommons.org/licenses/by-sa/3.0*>, *via Wikimedia Commons*
https://commons.wikimedia.org/wiki/File:Inca_Empire_South_America.png

To keep the leaders from revolting or conspiring against the centralized government, informers—a network of "secret police," if you will—were put in place to monitor local conditions in the regions they were assigned. These secret agents were also frequently sent to territories on the fringes of the empire to feel out how best to convince or coerce these neighboring peoples to join with the Incas.

Although many of these instances are referred to as overtures to join the empire, they are better described as "polite demands." The leaders of these neighboring tribes knew full well that to refuse an invitation to join the Inca Empire was tantamount to declaring war on them.

However, those who were subjugated didn't always have an easy go of it. Sure, they avoided open warfare with a powerful neighbor, but they also had to give up much of their identity in the process. Even the children of tribal leaders were expected to marry into the Inca royal line to prevent any future potential rebellion or discord. We may look back with scorn at such heavy-handed tactics today, but these tactics helped keep the Inca Empire firmly glued together.

One of the greatest wars of expansion undertaken by an Inca ruler was the clash against the Kingdom of Chimor to the north of Peru. The Kingdom of Chimor was challenged by Prince Túpac Inca Yupanqui in 1463, and the war continued until after his father's demise in 1471. Túpac Inca (also known as Topa Inca) became Sapa Inca and would rule over the empire.

After Túpac Inca Yupanqui died, his son, Huayna Capac, sat on the throne. Under his leadership, the expansion of the empire continued until it stretched across much of the western coast of South America. The Incas would hold onto this empire for the next few decades and seemed poised to do so for some time to come. But when they received a sudden interruption of intruders from overseas, everything would change.

Chapter 2 – The First Phase of the Spanish Conquest

"If you do not accept the yoke of the Church and the King of Spain—I will make war on you."

-Francisco Pizarro

The Spanish conquest of the Americas impacted the Incas before the two even faced off against each other. In the early 1520s, the scourge of smallpox, which the Spanish had been unintentionally spreading since they made landfall in Central America, had made its way to Inca territories, where it began to spread like wildfire.

As devastating as this illness was, the Spanish were not affected. They were blessed with a robust immune system used to fighting off smallpox, while natives in the Americas had never been exposed to it before. Since their immune system never had to deal with the disease before, they had no natural defenses against it. The invisible germs the Spanish spread often served as their forward guard, annihilating their potential enemies before they even went into battle.

And this was very much the case with the Incas. While the Spaniards had their hands full with subjecting the Aztecs of Mexico hundreds of miles away, smallpox germs managed to reach the edges of the Incas' territory. By 1524, the Inca royal family had been infected. Huayna Capac died from the illness in 1527, and his son and heir, Ninan Cuyochi, died shortly thereafter. Huayna Capac supposedly prophesized that the Inca Empire would be conquered by outsiders shortly before his passing. Such tales are hard to prove, but the legend that he had somehow prophesized the Incas' demise would later become widespread.

His passing led to a succession crisis, with his two remaining sons, Atahualpa and Huáscar, fighting it out to see who would become the paramount chief. The Inca Empire entered into a civil war, which made it easier for the Spanish conquistador Francisco Pizarro and his men to take over the Inca Empire. Ultimately, Atahualpa triumphed. He imprisoned his brother Huáscar, who was kept under close watch.

By 1531, Pizarro had established a kind of base camp on the coast of Peru. The locals had seen the giant wooden ships land and witnessed men with powerful steel swords, pikes, and guns. They also took note of the strange and wondrous beasts called horses.

Francisco Pizarro.
https://commons.wikimedia.org/wiki/File:Portrait_of_Francisco_Pizarro.jpg

All of these things led some to think these were not ordinary men but rather some sort of supernatural entity. This superstition led most of the locals to give these visitors a wide berth. However, the supposed supernatural qualities of the Spanish were dashed when a Spanish interpreter by the name of Cinquichara, who already had experience with the Spanish, briefed the Inca ruler as to what was going on.

Cinquichara insisted these interlopers were nothing more than regular human beings who just so happened to be equipped with powerful weapons. Cinquichara insisted that they were just ordinary men who were mean and nasty. Many reports had come in that the invaders had made many grievous trespasses against the locals, and Cinquichara confirmed as much. He advised the king that the Spaniards should be dispatched at once. He even went as far as to suggest that they should be "burned as they slept."

If the Inca ruler had taken his translator up on this advice, history might have played out differently. To be sure, even if these conquistadors were snuffed out, more would likely come, but decisive action might have delayed the inevitable toppling of this great civilization. The Inca ruler dithered, and Pizarro embarked upon a propaganda campaign to convince the Inca leader that he was on his side.

He sent an envoy led by Hernando de Soto to seek a direct audience with the Inca ruler. This audience was granted, but rather than opening up their society to the Spaniards, the Inca emperor stated that he was displeased with the way locals had been treated by the Spanish. Pizarro and his men insisted that wasn't the case and that the king was, in fact, mistaken.

Considering that anything other than conciliatory apologies might have had the Inca ruler signal his men to kill the Spaniards on the spot, it is not surprising they took this tactic. Atahualpa ultimately let them go, but his mercy would come back to haunt him soon enough.

It was then arranged for Atahualpa and his entourage to meet with the Spanish where they had camped in the village of Cajamarca in November 1532.

Emperor Atahualpa came to the town square in good faith, but the Spaniards were planning an ambush. Instead of greeting Atahualpa and his men when they arrived, Francisco Pizarro and a small group of men hid in nearby buildings centered around the town square.

It would later be learned that Atahualpa was aware of what the Spaniards were doing due to the fact that he had sent some spies into the town square ahead of time. It was reported to him that the Spaniards were so terrified of him and his entourage's approach that they were hiding in fear. This interpretation of events was only partially correct. It is true the Spaniards were hiding, and it is true that many of them were terrified. They were incredibly outnumbered and had just been ordered by Pizarro to take on thousands of legions of Incas (however, most of them were unarmed when they entered the city).

The Spanish were frightened, but they didn't have much of a choice but to follow Pizarro's orders. Unless they suddenly rebelled against their commander and fled into the wilderness—which likely meant capture or death—they would have to do what they were told, no matter how scared they might have been.

The Spanish were holed up in the buildings not out of fear but in preparation to rush out and ambush the Inca ruler. As Atahualpa's entourage approached, he was even heard shouting for the Spaniards to come out.

Finally, two of them did come out, but it was not Pizarro or his troops. The only two to emerge into the town square were a priest and his translator. They were Dominican friar Father Vicente de Valverde and a local who had become a new convert to Christianity and served as a translator.

The priest used his translator to address the king and began to question him about his religious beliefs. Father Valverde explained Christianity and gave Atahualpa a chance to convert.

Francisco Pizarro knew that the Inca armed forces could only be adequately mobilized under their absolutist monarch. He knew that if Atahualpa was seized and put under his direct control, he could essentially rule the Incas by using Atahualpa as his own personal puppet.

But before any action was taken, Pizarro had to create a pretext first. The Spaniards, you see, were conquistadors who had sworn to promote Christianity, whether by force or persuasion. In 1513, a law was passed called the Requerimiento, which required the conquistadors to give the new people groups they encountered the chance to convert to Christianity before subjecting them to conquest.

But the Requerimiento actually goes deeper than that, stating that the pope, as God's representative on Earth, had given the Spanish Crown jurisdiction over this part of the world. Thus, it was imperative for all within this jurisdiction to submit not only to Christianity but also to the Spanish Crown. In other words, this was a required reading of rights to the newly discovered peoples in the Americas.

As it pertains to Atahualpa, he was informed he had the right to become a Christian and accept deference to the Spanish king as his paramount chief, or he had the right to be subjected to the Spanish sword as a continuation of the holy war they had been waging ever since the start of the Reconquista.

It is intriguing to note that the same demands that were being foisted upon natives by the Spanish are very much similar to the demands that the Ottoman Turks gave at the gates of Vienna when Islamic armies nearly took the city. Before engaging in combat, the Turks read the Austrians their "rights," demanding they submit to Islam or face the sultan's wrath. Atahualpa was put in a very similar situation by the Spanish. They were basically saying, "Convert or else."

As mentioned, Spain had just come out of the Reconquista, in which the Spaniards had struggled for centuries to reclaim or "reconquer" Spanish territory that had been lost to Muslim invaders. As they fought holy wars to push Islamic forces out of Iberia, Spain developed a particularly militant form of Catholic Christianity. For the Spanish, it had become a zero-sum game of Christians and non-Christians. If someone was a non-Christian—as the Incas were—they were an enemy of God and, therefore, an enemy to the Spanish Crown.

It might be hard for us to understand such things today in our (for the most part) religiously tolerant world, but this was indeed the mindset Pizarro and his men had. Even though they were eager to topple the Incas, they couldn't do so until they at least tried to see if they could get the Inca king to convert. It's hard to know if Atahualpa could even grasp what this priest was saying, but if he did and if he accepted the Christian faith, we can only imagine how different history would have been.

It is likely the Spaniards were waiting for the Inca emperor's rejection of Christianity, not his embrace of the religion. If the mighty Inca emperor suddenly declared, "Yes! I believe in Christianity! I want to be a Christian!" Pizarro probably would have been disappointed since he would have lost all pretext to attack the Incas.

If Atahualpa knew what the Spaniards were up to, he could have been crafty enough to pretend to convert. This would have given the Incas some time to prepare for a larger war before the Spaniards launched an inquisition into whether Atahualpa was really a Christian or not.

But this was not how history played out. After the priest's lecture, Atahualpa, bristling with anger, demanded to see the priest's prayer book. The Inca did not have books of their own, but they had something called a quipu, which was an elaborate system of knotted cords that they used to convey and record important information.

Some have suggested that perhaps the translator, not having a word for book since such things did not exist in the Inca world, used the word "quipu" as an equivalent. So, one can only imagine that when the translator conveyed the priest's message, stating that he held in his hands a quipu that contained the words of God, Atahualpa was quite curious to see what it said.

The priest handed the book up to Atahualpa, who had remained seated in a litter, which was held aloft by his servants. After taking the book in his hands, the Inca ruler appeared quite puzzled and began to turn it upside down as if he were trying to figure out how it was used.

Finally, he flipped through the pages, but seeing that it was just paper with letters printed on their surface, he became dismayed. There was no knotted cord conveying great information, and as far as the Inca ruler could tell, this was certainly no quipu. Atahualpa apparently didn't see the point of the object and tossed the Bible on the ground. This was his answer to the Requerimiento.

Some later accounts contend that Atahualpa then began issuing orders for his men to prepare to seize the Spaniards and punish them for all of the trouble they had caused. The translator retrieved the Bible for Father Valverde, and the two rushed back to where the Spaniards were holed up. Valverde is said to have shouted, "Come out! Come out, Christians! Come at these enemy dogs who reject the things of God! The chief has thrown the book of holy law to the ground!"

Father Valverde clearly believed (no matter how misguided) that one was either on the side of God or against God. Since the Incas practiced another faith, Valverde assumed they were in league with the devil himself. After Valverde supposedly shouted these words, Pizarro gave the signal to Pedro de Candia, who was on the other side of the square, lodged where the cannons had been readied. The planned ambush was about to begin.

As arranged beforehand, Pedro began firing his cannons into the assembled Inca entourage. The loud explosions stunned the Incas, and the countless bodies suddenly spurting blood from the stumps that used to be heads, arms, and legs after the cannonballs collided into them brought understandable terror. Despite the huge numbers of

Atahualpa's army, panic began to set in. The Spanish continued to push their advance by staging a cavalry charge immediately after this initial volley rang out. Suddenly, Spanish troops on horseback came charging into the center of the Inca positions, hacking, stabbing, and slashing their way through the crowd.

Although Atahualpa's entourage tried to protect him, the Spaniards surged forward and grabbed him. They rode off with their royal hostage, ready to begin their game of manipulation. The Inca army was confused about what to do and panicked as the Spaniards continued to shoot and hack them to pieces. The Incas fled but were hampered by the narrow exits of the plaza. This situation was not alleviated until a mob of thousands of Incas managed to knock down a wall, providing a larger escape route. Even then, the Spanish doggedly pursued them, stabbing as many in the back as they could as they fled from their sight.

Atahualpa was held for ransom. Atahualpa told Pizarro, with the help of a translator, that he could give the Spanish all the gold and silver they ever wanted if they would just let him go. But the Spaniards were never going to do any such thing. Much has been made about the greediness of Francisco Pizarro and his men in this regard, and they certainly were.

But there was another reason for their unwillingness to spare Atahualpa. Pizarro knew that the second he let the Inca leader go, the full might of the Inca army would be rallied against him. If Pizarro had let the Inca ruler go, he would have loaded up his horses with half the empire's treasury and then began the long trek back to the Spanish-controlled coast. Would Atahualpa really just have sat back and allowed these Spaniards to waltz off into the sunset laden with treasure after abducting him and killing thousands of his subjects? Pizarro never would have gotten out of Peru alive.

No matter what Pizarro might have promised or pledged to the Inca ruler, he clearly had no real intention of ever letting his hostage go. The restraining hand of the still-living Atahualpa kept the Inca armies from attacking.

In the meantime, the Spaniards received all of the treasure they had demanded. To get it, they allowed Atahualpa to communicate with messengers so they could make arrangements to procure wealth from all corners of the empire.

This communication was achieved through a system of relay runners, which were situated throughout the empire. This system allowed

Atahualpa to send a message all the way to Cuzco in just a few days. However, the Spaniards did not know that Atahualpa also issued an order for his brother, Huáscar, who was still being held, to be put to death. He did this out of fear that his brother and his supporters would use his compromised position against him and launch a coup to seize power.

This was a selfish act on Atahualpa's part. Perhaps if he had refrained from killing his own brother, the Incas would have rallied behind Huáscar and kept the Inca Empire intact. Even better, he could have authorized his brother's release, and the Incas could have immediately waged war on the Spanish through Huáscar. But instead, he had his brother killed.

The Spaniards eventually learned of what happened, and they used this fratricide as an excuse to have Atahualpa executed. Francisco Pizarro and his men had already been informed of the imprisoned Huáscar through their own interpreters and had looked forward to having him brought into their custody as well. However, when Pizarro first heard of what had happened, he did not immediately protest. When Atahualpa lied and claimed that his guards had killed his brother without his orders, Pizarro seemed to let the matter drop.

In the meantime, Pizarro and his men got to know Atahualpa fairly well. They even taught him how to play chess, a game the Inca royal apparently was quite fond of and became an expert at. Ironically, the game of chess that he played very much symbolized the situation he was in. He was constantly trying to anticipate the movements of his captors and what his next move should be.

Atahualpa was initially allowed to have his servants tend to his every need, allowing him to live a life of luxury even while in captivity. One of his guards, a certain Pedro Pizarro (a cousin of Francisco Pizarro), would later recall the stunning sight of seeing servant women feed the king from their own hands. At one point, one accidentally dropped a morsel of food, and it landed on Atahualpa's royal robes. Not showing any mercy to the foibles of his servants, the Inca royal struck the woman and then got up to change his clothes. He returned in an extravagant, dark brown cloak.

The guard brushed up against the cloak and was amazed at how soft it was. Pedro asked Atahualpa what the cloak was made of and was stunned to learn that it was composed entirely of the skins of vampire bats. Vampire bats are one of the largest bats in the known world and the only bats that are known to occasionally bite people to feed.

Amazed at how the skins of such a dangerous creature had been procured in such large numbers, Pedro asked how it was done. Concerned about his own people whose forced labor had brought him the magnificent robes he wore, the Inca ruler shrugged and said something to the effect of, "What else did they have to do other than catch bats and make clothes?" Unquestioning subservience to the elite was the Inca Empire's greatest strength and its greatest weakness.

The fact that the people of Peru would do anything that Atahualpa said was what the Spaniards were banking on all along. They knew they had nothing to fear from the vast Inca army that otherwise would have crushed them as long as they had Atahualpa in their possession.

The Spaniards were eager to get the gold that Atahualpa had promised them in his desperate bid to secure his freedom. On May 13th, 1533, a few of Pizarro's men who had left with a legion of Inca troops returned with many of the spoils. To the astonishment of local Incas in Cuzco, these men raided the most sacred temples in the Inca capital, taking all of the precious silver and gold ornaments and stripping gold-plated walls bare. Upon their arrival back at the camp at Cajamarca, the Spanish camp had been reinforced with over a hundred more Spanish warriors fresh from the coast.

It is said that Atahualpa became noticeably upset upon the arrival of these fresh Spanish faces. He apparently realized that the arrival of this one group of outsiders was not an outside event. Previously, he had convinced himself that Pizarro and his men were a rare group of bandits who would be gone after getting their gold.

He was also quite distressed when he learned that Hernando Pizarro—Francisco Pizarro's brother—was leading a group of men with pack animals loaded up with treasure (all of the precious Inca artifacts had been quickly melted into gold and silver bars for easy transport) to ships waiting on the coast so they could sail with all of their loot back to Spain.

Not only did it seem that Francisco Pizarro was not keeping his promise of releasing him, but the fact that Hernando was leaving severely disturbed Atahualpa, who had personally befriended him. It appears as if Hernando was the nicer of the Pizarro brothers, and Atahualpa viewed him as his own personal protector. Many years later, Hernando would claim that the Inca ruler had actually begged him to go with him on his trip out of fear that he would be killed after he was gone.

The elder Pizarro—Francisco—was already building up his pretext for just that. Atahualpa did not have to wait long for his death. Shortly after Hernando's departure, a local-chief-turned-informant told Francisco that he had received word that a rescue attempt for Atahualpa was already under way.

This local Inca administrator claimed that Atahualpa's "northern army" was heading south toward Cajamarca. Further incensing Francisco Pizarro, the chief told him that he would be the first to be targeted and killed. The chief claimed that some 200,000 of these troops were on their way, along with an auxiliary force of 30,000 Caribs.

The idea of the Caribs arriving to help the Incas was particularly frightening for the Spaniards since they had encountered this tribe previously during their exploits in the Caribbean. The Caribs were known for practicing cannibalism, and the Inca chief apparently intimated that they would likely "eat human flesh" if they were unleashed upon Pizarro and his men.

As soon as Francisco Pizarro heard all of this, he set up a strong guard around Cajamarca before inquiring with Atahualpa about these developments. If Atahualpa was playing a game of chess, Francisco was seeking to block his move with a proverbial checkmate.

However, upon being confronted with this supposed plot, Atahualpa denied being involved. It is said that despite the dire situation he was in, the Inca ruler remained stoic and calm, matter-of-factly stating that such a thing could only be done upon his orders and that he had ordered no such thing. He then challenged Pizarro to see for himself if this was the case.

After his interrogation of Atahualpa, Pizarro met with his inner circle, where it was vigorously debated what should be done. The results were nonconclusive. There were some who wanted to get rid of the Inca ruler and have him executed, but others insisted it would be better if he were kept alive. So, they decided to wait things out and see what happened.

In the meantime, Francisco Pizarro sent Hernando de Soto with a small group of men to ride north and see for themselves if a massive army was actually approaching. But shortly after de Soto's party left, a sailor named Pedro de Anadel suddenly broke up a card game Francisco was having with his men to declare that a massive Inca army was just a few miles from their camp.

This was not seen by Pedro; apparently, his native servant and translator had seen it. Francisco Pizarro immediately turned to the translator and demanded to hear his account. Pizarro found the words of the translator so convincing that he truly believed that an Inca army was about to descend. As such, he and his men decided they needed to dispatch with the Inca emperor as soon as possible.

But for what reason? These supposedly Christian men did not want to think of themselves as cold-blooded murderers (even though many today would likely describe them as such), so they needed to have a reason behind the execution of the Inca emperor. The most obvious in their minds was charges of treason. The logic behind this is about as convoluted as can be, but from their perspective, the Inca ruler had somehow betrayed their trust and committed treason against the Spanish Crown by sending an army to their encampment.

Most today would view such an interpretation of events as utterly absurd. The Spaniards had trespassed into Atahualpa's domain, ambushed him, and taken him prisoner. Wouldn't it be within his rights to order his own rescue, especially considering the fact that the Spaniards didn't seem to be fulfilling their pledge to release him? But the Spaniards didn't see it this way.

They viewed Atahualpa as having betrayed them, and on top of these supposed charges of treason, they also added the charge of his brother's murder, whom Atahualpa had ordered to be killed. After Atahualpa's "trial," the predetermined sentence was, of course, death. On July 26th, 1533, a weeping Atahualpa was led outside and tied to a stake. Wood was gathered around his feet. Father Valverde was summoned, and he stood before the Inca ruler, attempting one last time to convert this "heretic" to Christianity.

As much as we might cringe with horror at some of the things these men did, the fact they made such an effort to convert Atahualpa is an indication of just how firm their beliefs were (no matter how warped they were). For even after everything else, it was viewed as a necessity to make one last attempt to convert the Inca ruler to Christianity.

Father Valverde, the same man who had first confronted the Inca ruler at Cajamarca with his "quipu" from which he said God himself spoke, stood over the weeping Atahualpa and again preached to him about the Christian religion, informing him that God would pardon him of all of his sins if he would just accept the sacrifice made by Jesus Christ.

It is unclear how much Atahualpa might have understood what was being said. Father Valverde's words were being translated through an interpreter, but the concepts might have been too foreign to grasp, especially when staring death right in the face. Some have even wondered if perhaps Atahualpa thought he was being told that his mortal life would be spared if he converted when the priest was actually referring to his immortal soul. At any rate, when the priest indicated that if he converted, he would be spared from being burned at the stake and would instead be "garroted" or strangled by way of a rope around his neck, Atahualpa became more interested.

The last thing an Inca wanted was to be burned to ashes. The Inca tradition was to preserve the body after death. Just like the Egyptians, their kings were often mummified, ostensibly believing that they would one day be resurrected. Interestingly enough, this is identical to Christian beliefs.

Although modern Christians might endlessly speak about the "Rapture," the concept of the Rapture (a term not even in the Bible) did not become a part of Christian discourse until the 19th century. Prior to this, the main thrust of Christianity was the resurrection of the dead. Folks weren't waiting around to be raptured; they were waiting to be resurrected. Just as Jesus was physically resurrected from the dead, Christians preached that all would be resurrected in the end times.

Christians would be resurrected and experience great rewards and paradise, whereas the unsaved would be resurrected to suffer damnation and punishment. It was for this reason that Christian authorities developed the habit of having supposed heretics burned at the stake since they believed they were denying them the chance to take part in the resurrection.

The notion of keeping the body intact for an impeding resurrection was something that Atahualpa already believed, and so he readily agreed with the priest to convert. The priest quickly baptized the Inca ruler into the faith.

As Atahualpa's executioners prepared the rope that would end his life, the priest gave Atahualpa his last rites according to the full tradition of the Catholic Church. One can only imagine the full-on drama that took place, with Atahualpa openly weeping, his executioners readying the implements of his death, and the black-robed priest, Father

Valverde, reading the last and final rites of the newly converted Inca ruler.

Valverde was heard loudly proclaiming the scripture, "Yea, though I walk through the valley of the shadow of death, I will fear no evil, for You art with me." The executioners dutifully tightened the rope around the Inca ruler's neck, the pressure quickly stopping Atahualpa from breathing. Mere seconds later, as oxygen left his brain, he perished. After an abbreviated ceremony, the Inca ruler was buried in an unmarked grave. The Spaniards likely intended for the location to remain undisclosed until perhaps resurrection day.

The Funerals of Inca Atahualpa by Luis Montero, a Peruvian painter.
https://commons.wikimedia.org/wiki/File:Luis_Montero_-_The_Funerals_of_Inca_Atahualpa_-_Google_Art_Project.jpg

The supposed army sent to rescue the now-deceased emperor never arrived. A few days after Atahualpa was executed, Hernando de Soto, who had been sent to observe what was happening in the north, rushed into the camp on horseback to breathlessly inform Pizarro that they had seen no sign whatsoever of any massive mobilization of troops on the horizon.

It was then that Pizarro must have realized that he had been misinformed. Those who whispered the rumors about Atahualpa's rescue perhaps had other motives in mind. Maybe they wanted to incur the wrath of the Spaniards against the Inca king for their own personal grievances. At any rate, Francisco Pizarro realized too late that it was the Incan emperor who had been betrayed by these false reports and not the other way around.

It is said that Pizarro, immediately betrayed by his own guilty conscience, wept before de Soto, who scolded Pizarro for killing the Atahualpa for no reason.

The death of the puppet king opened the door for an open revolt against the Spaniards. Even without Atahualpa's fleet-footed messengers, word traveled fast from Cajamarca that Atahualpa was dead. Soon, a very real Incan army would be mobilized against the Spaniards.

As such, the Spaniards had to quickly take on an attitude of "what's done is done," and in order to ensure that they were not slaughtered, they had to pull together their resources and act quickly. An armed cavalry was put together under the charge of Hernando de Soto and sent hurtling toward the Inca capital of Cuzco. They reached the gates of Cuzco on November 14th, 1533, to find Atahualpa's army being led by Quisquis (his name is also commonly spelled as Quizquiz). Quisquis, knowing that Atahualpa was dead, was now free from any restraints that might have held him back and ordered his troops to attack the invading Spaniards.

Although the Spanish were incredibly outnumbered, the Spaniards, who were on horseback and wearing body armor, outmatched the Inca foot soldiers. The Incas' infantrymen were equipped with wooden maces topped with bronze or stone heads. Against other tribal adversaries, they could use these to bash in their opponents. But even if they could reach the heads of these horse-riding interlopers, the mace would simply bounce off the Spaniards' helmets. Stones and arrows hurled at the intruders were equally ineffective since they bounced off their armor.

To be sure, the Spaniards were battered and bruised from this onslaught, but the Incas were unable to inflict lethal wounds. The Inca troops, in the meantime, were being killed by Spanish swords left and right.

Perhaps if Quisquis had understood how the Spanish fought, he could have prepared a more effective strategy to use against them. If they could have simply overwhelmed the Spaniards and pulled them from their horses, they likely would not have survived. The Spaniards' guns and, even more importantly, their swords would be ineffective once they were on the ground with hundreds of Incas throwing themselves on top of them. This would have ended the Spanish quest to topple the Incas (at least in this go-round), but that is not what happened.

The Incas ferociously battered the mounted Spanish knights without much impact until the sun went down. There was then a brief truce, with both sides returning to their camps. However, Quisquis apparently concluded that the struggle against these invaders was futile, as he ordered his army to retreat quietly under cover of darkness. The Spaniards would not realize the army had left the field until the next morning.

In the meantime, Pizarro and another contingent of reinforcements arrived on the scene. Pizarro had arrived just in time to lead the whole Spanish contingent into an entirely undefended Cuzco.

One needs to take the power politics of the Incas into account to understand what happened next. Ever since the civil war had erupted, in which Atahualpa defeated his brother, Atahualpa's army had been occupying Cuzco. The local people who had previously supported Atahualpa's brother Huáscar were naturally resentful of this fact.

Francisco Pizarro was aware of this situation and used it to present himself and his cohorts as liberators. He also had another ace up his sleeve—another royal heir. Pizarro had come into contact with the surviving brother of Atahualpa and Huáscar, Manco Inca Yupanqui. This younger brother of the Inca ruler was named after arguably the greatest Inca of them all—Manco **Cápac, the founder.**

An image of Manco Cápac, the founder of the Inca Empire.
https://commons.wikimedia.org/wiki/File:Brooklyn_Museum_-_Manco_Capac,_First_Inca,_1_of_14_Portraits_of_Inca_Kings_-_overall.jpg

As mentioned earlier, the original Manco shoved his golden staff into the ground to found an empire. Now the question was could this new Manco hold on to it? With Manco Inca under his thumb, Pizarro and his men sought to convince the stunned and shell-shocked populace of Cuzco that the Spaniards not only came in peace but had also arrived to place the rightful ruler on the throne.

So, Manco Inca became the new puppet ruler of the Spaniards. The first order they gave Manco was for him to build his own army of Inca troops to better defend the capital from what remained of Atahualpa's old army. Manco, who had suffered at the hands of Quisquis's troops, readily complied. Manco raised an army, and then a combined Inca and Spanish force was sent to take on Quisquis's men.

The battle was devastating for Quisquis, and many of his subordinate officers soon made it clear that they would not carry on this fight. As such, Quisquis and those who remained loyal to him retreated to the northern stronghold of Quito. Quisquis would eventually develop some rather sound strategies for defeating the invaders. At one point, when confronted by Spanish reinforcements that had arrived in the north, he staged a successful ambush.

Quisquis had his troops situated on higher ground, and they were able to waylay the Spaniards from above, rendering the mobility and height provided by their horses useless. During this skirmish, a large number of Spanish troops were killed. Nevertheless, Quisquis's ability to command his demoralized troops began to break down. Soon, they were openly revolting against him.

In the past, mutiny among the Inca ranks was met with death as punishment. Quisquis began threatening as much, but instead of him being able to punish the mutineers, they punished him. One of his officers, whose name comes down to us as Huaypalcon, hurled a spear at the general, striking him in the chest. This was apparently the cue to let loose. Several warriors descended upon their former leader, each striking him with clubs and battle axes until he was no longer breathing.

With the threat of the northern army neutralized, Pizarro and his men attended Manco Inca's official coronation. Pizarro took this special occasion of the crowning of a new Inca emperor as an opportunity to read the Inca people their "rights." During this grand ceremony, Pizarro took center stage and read out the Requerimiento, the requirements that the Spanish Crown expected of the Incans.

This was the same script that had been read aloud to Atahualpa prior to him tossing a Bible on the ground and being seized by Spanish troops. This time around, Manco Inca and his followers received the words with glee. Whether they fully understood what it meant to become a Christian or be subject to both the pope and the faraway Spanish king is unclear, but they apparently understood how the Spaniards wished for them to respond, and they did not disappoint.

After hearing the requirements read aloud by an interpreter, the Incas broke out in cheers. The young Inca ruler, Manco Inca, then rose from his throne and embraced Pizarro as if he were his own brother. If only this brotherly love could have lasted. Tragically, this would not be the case.

Chapter 3 – The Last Days of the Incan Empire

"When his [Atahualpa's squadrons] were formed so that they covered fields, and when he had seated himself on a litter, he began to proceed. Two thousand Indians marched before him, sweeping the [stone paved] road on which he traveled. Half of his troops marched on one side of the road and half on the other, with neither using the road itself. So great was the amount of furniture of gold and silver which they bore, that it was a marvel to observe how it all glittered beneath the sun."

-Pedro Pizarro

Shortly after Manco Inca's coronation came to its conclusion, he was installed on the throne at Cuzco. The Spaniards then set about creating their own base on the Pacific coast, which was finished in January 1535. This settlement would ultimately become Lima, the future capital of Peru. The settling of Lima by primarily Spanish Europeans would set a precedent. From this point forward, Lima would be flooded by European immigrants, while Cuzco would remain populated primarily by native Peruvians.

Pizarro appointed conquistador Diego de Almagro as lieutenant governor, placing him in charge of Cuzco. Almagro was friendly with Manco Inca, and for a time, a sense of stability could be felt in Cuzco. However, on July 2nd, 1535, de Almagro was suddenly called to leave on an expedition farther south, and Francisco put his two younger brothers, Juan and Gonzalo Pizarro, in charge.

Diego de Almagro.
https://commons.wikimedia.org/wiki/File:Diego_de_Almagro.JPG

These two young and somewhat immature men proved themselves to be absolutely ruthless. Without the more sober conquistadors around to keep them in check, they ran riot all through Cuzco. Acting like mini-dictators, they demanded silver, gold, and, even more problematic, women. You see, these young men were notorious drunks and womanizers. If they saw a woman they wanted, they expected to have her.

This was scandalous enough for the Inca elite, but when Juan Pizarro began to demand some quality time with Manco Inca's own wife, the Incas were pushed to their limits. Finally, the Pizarro brothers had broken a sacred rule that Manco Inca could not meekly overlook. Manco Inca was understandably frustrated with the exploitation of his Spanish handlers, and he finally lost his patience. In November 1535, he took the first concerted step in what would be a long struggle of resistance.

Around this time, he secretly convened a group of high-ranking Incas and made it clear that he wanted to stand up against the Spaniards. His words set in motion an empire-wide mobilization effort. His attempts would be briefly thwarted when his plans were uncovered by the Spaniards. Manco Inca was thrown in prison by the younger Pizarro brothers.

Even so, his words had already set in motion the mobilization of the Incas. Soon, sporadic uprisings began to take place. Many of them seemed almost random, but they were all a part of the growing effort to shake off the Spaniards.

Manco Inca was freed when the older Pizarro brother (second to only Francisco himself), Hernando, returned from Spain. Hernando arrived in January of 1536 and was disgusted to hear of how terribly his younger brothers had treated Manco Inca and the rest of the Incas. Hernando had express orders from the king of Spain, who was also the Holy Roman emperor, Charles V, that Manco Inca should not only be treated well but also rewarded for his cooperation with Spain. Obviously, this had not been the case. Hernando sought to set things right and freed Manco Inca, restoring him to the throne.

Gonzalo and Juan Pizarro likely feared Manco Inca might exact some sort of revenge on them. However, despite their protests, Hernando insisted that Manco Inca would remain free. He also assured them that Manco Inca had promised he would not cause them any trouble. Manco Inca knew that he was dealing with some rather duplicitous characters and, at this point, had no problem with telling some lies of his own.

In reality, Manco Inca had no intention of cooperating. He had a desire for vengeance burning deep in his soul. Instead of seeking diplomatic relations, he began to secretly arrange the final steps toward an outright revolt against Spanish rule. Large armed groups slowly made their way to the capital, apparently taking their time to avoid the worst of the rainy season. On April 18th, 1536, Manco Inca made his move.

He asked Hernando Pizarro if he and his high priest, which was called a *villac umu*, could head off on a pilgrimage to the site where his father, the great Inca Huayna Capac, was buried to perform an important religious ceremony. Perhaps Hernando was still feeling guilty for Manco Inca's previous mistreatment since he readily agreed. But Manco Inca was not merely paying respects to his father's tomb; he was linking up to be at the head of a massive army.

This group of well over 100,000 troops descended on Cuzco and encircled it. In the meantime, another detachment of a large body of troops was sent to Lima to ensure that reinforcements from Francisco Pizarro would not be forthcoming.

Hernando and the two younger Pizarro brothers were panicking. Hernando realized the full gravity of the situation and was upset over his decision to allow Manco Inca to leave.

To test the mettle of the advancing Incas, Hernando led several cavalry charges out of the city. They were met by a virtual storm of stones and arrows. In one instance, Hernando's group was even surrounded and very nearly annihilated just outside Cuzco's gates. Although Hernando led his men out of this near-complete disaster, at least one of his men did not make it.

It was recorded that a conquistador by the name of Francisco Mejia was knocked off his horse in the chaos and was immediately seized by the mob of Incas. Soon, his severed head was being raised up over the walls of Cuzco to taunt the beleaguered Spaniards. Shortly thereafter, the siege entered into an even more deadly phase when the Incas began to set fire to the roofs of houses in the city. The fire quickly spread, and a blazing inferno soon erupted.

It was Manco Inca's intention to either force the Spaniards out of his capital or burn it to the ground with them in it. Manco Inca's desire to destroy his enemies was perhaps best demonstrated by the burning of Cuzco. How often had the cruel Gonzalo Pizarro threatened to burn him alive? Manco Inca was merely returning the favor.

Sick of literally putting out fires, Hernando Pizarro decided to lead his men out in a desperate counterattack against the forces arrayed against them. As the final battle played out within Cuzco, Manco Inca's forces demonstrated they had perfected a couple of strategies. First of all, they realized that height was their greatest advantage against the Spaniards on horseback. Whenever possible, they scaled walls and roofs and showered the Spaniards and their horses with stones, arrows, and whatever else they could hurl down upon them.

Perhaps even more decisively, they brought along an impressive weapon that the Spaniards knew nothing about. It was a device that consisted of smooth round stones inserted into leather pouches that were connected to a cord that spanned about a yard long. The Spanish called the device a bola due to the ball-like implements. Whatever it was called, the weapon was good at taking out horses.

The warrior who wielded the bola would basically swing it rapidly over their head and then hurl it at the legs of the horses. The balls would then wrap tightly around the horse's legs. Incas had previously used the instrument as a hunting weapon to take down deer. Someone eventually had the brilliant idea to use it to take down the Spanish cavalry. Initially, these efforts were wildly successful, but the grizzled Spaniards, who were veterans of countless wars in Europe and beyond, quickly adapted their strategies.

Realizing the threat, the Spaniards simply made sure that those on horseback had a couple of foot soldiers nearby. That way, they could quickly steady and cut bound horses loose before they toppled over.

Hernando made the fateful decision to take on the main encampment of Incas, which had holed up in an impressive fortress called Sacsayhuamán, located just outside of the city. The fortress, which had only been sparsely occupied by the Spaniards, had actually been abandoned upon the Incas' approach. Manco Inca had since made this mighty fortress his headquarters. Hernando realized that if he could reach Manco Inca, it would be over. So, Hernando sent his cavalry charging through the mob directly to the fortress. They were initially stalled by the usual stones and arrows hurled at them, but with the help of some old-fashioned siege ladders, they soon engineered a major breakthrough.

The ruins of Sacsayhuamán.
Apollo , CC BY 2.0 <https://creativecommons.org/licenses/by/2.0>, via Wikimedia Commons
https://commons.wikimedia.org/wiki/File:Sacsayhuaman_-_51188929520.jpg

They braved the stone hail that pummeled them and climbed up the fortress walls. This charge was led by the younger brother, Juan Pizarro. Juan was not in the best shape at the time. During a previous skirmish, he had been hit in the face with a stone, which severely injured his jaw, causing painful swelling. This prevented him from being able to wear a helmet without causing great pain.

As such, he tossed his helmet to the side and refused to wear one at all. In the coming struggle with the defenders of the citadel, this would prove to be a crucial factor in his downfall. The first line of defense that Juan Pizarro and his group encountered at the fortress was a narrow pass filled with stones. This part of the citadel was unguarded at the time, but it was a laborious task to remove all of these bits of masonry.

Their efforts alerted the defenders as to what they were up to, and once the Spanish got through into the courtyard, they were met with a hail of stones, arrows, and darts. This onslaught stopped them in their tracks. Still, Juan was determined to make some kind of headway against Manco Inca's fortress stronghold. The Spaniards rallied and charged into the center of the defenders, making their long-range missiles useless at close range, and hacked through them until they were able to insert themselves right in the middle of the courtyard.

The defenders were forced up onto the second tier of the fortress, where they, once again, held the high ground. They attempted to press their advantage by raining down death on the Spaniards below. During this melee, Juan Pizarro was struck in the head with a huge rock. Although he would be dragged off the battlefield and linger in a semi-conscious state of agony for a few more days, he died from his wounds.

Hernando Pizarro took over the assault, heading to the fortress while leaving the most troublesome Pizarro of them all—Gonzalo—in charge of Cuzco's defense. This time around, siege ladders were brought to stand up against the walls, and the Spaniards used them to charge up onto parapet after parapet.

The Inca defenders were fierce and used stones, arrows, and darts to deal death to those who stood against them. However, they had problems dealing with strong Spanish armor and steel swords. It took some time, but the Spaniards fought their way level by level through the fortress until they were finally able to seize it for themselves.

But despite what appeared to be a terrible defeat for the Incas, the other Inca contingent under Quizo Yupanqui, which had positioned itself on the road to Lima, was about to score some of the greatest Inca victories.

Francisco Pizarro had learned of what was happening in Cuzco and sent over reinforcements. Quizo expected as much and developed a great strategy: he waited for the Spanish troops to enter the narrow passes and then had his troops block both ends of the pass.

He had more troops positioned up above, and they unleashed a barrage of huge boulders. The huge rocks slammed into horses and men. The panicked Spaniards tried to break free of the trap they had walked into, but they could not. They were stabbed, hacked, and pummeled to death. Quizo repeated these same tactics on the next batch of troops to emerge. Hundreds of Spaniards died, and it is believed that a third of Pizarro's men were wiped out.

However, the greatest disaster was yet to come. Francisco Pizarro had actually grabbed another of Manco Inca's long-lost kin, a brother named Cusi Rimac. Francisco planned to stage another coronation for another puppet emperor. This Inca ruler-in-waiting, along with a group of Inca notables and a contingent of Spanish guards, were sent to Cuzco.

Little did they know that this potential puppet ruler was well aware of what was happening and had already secretly informed Manco Inca that he would do everything he could to fight for him. Cusi Rimac lived up to his promise. When this group was ambushed, the would-be puppet and his followers turned on the bewildered Spanish. The Spaniards fought against the Incas from within and without, and they were annihilated.

Feeling as if they must somehow break the siege they were under, Hernando de Soto decided to go ahead and take the fight to Manco Inca himself. He gathered together a small group of cavalry units and charged off to Manco Inca's personal fortress, located at a place called Ollantaytambo. With a decisive conclusion to their struggle in mind, Hernando and his men charged into the Yucay Valley.

In order to cross the rugged plains, they had to follow the Yucay River and were required to cross it several times. At each crossing, they were waylaid by hidden Inca fighters, who hurled stones at them from all sides. As they traveled farther down the plain, they also began to face the threat of Amazonian warriors, who mercilessly fired arrows at them.

These warriors were from the wild interior of the Amazon and were completely unknown to the Spaniards at the time. They had been tapped by Manco Inca as a kind of auxiliary mercenary force. They used arrows with finely sharpened bamboo points, and their aim and accuracy were extraordinary. Even so, unless they managed to hit the Spaniards right in the face, the Spaniards' armor protected them from much of this onslaught. They managed to make their way to Manco Inca's fortress, but a fresh horde of thousands of fighters was suddenly unleashed. The Incas drove the Spaniards back with their ferocity.

It was at this moment that Manco Inca used a secret weapon: he ordered his men to redirect the flow of nearby canals so that river water flooded right into the plain. The Incas were expert canal builders, so it is quite intriguing that they would use their marvelous ability to redirect water as a weapon against their enemies. At any rate, the plain was soon flooded. Before Hernando and company knew quite what was happening, they were in water up to their horse's bridle. The situation was untenable, and they were forced to flee.

The harried Spaniards were then hunted and hounded by their opponents all the way back to Cuzco. Once again, the only thing that saved them from utter annihilation was their high perch on their horses and the strong armor that they wore.

Manco Inca's famous general Quizo, who had so effectively destroyed the Spaniards, was given literal marching orders to lay siege to Lima. In fact, he was ordered to annihilate everyone within the city walls, save for Francisco Pizarro himself, whom Manco wished to take prisoner.

Manco likely desired to have the greatest revenge by reversing his situation on the Spaniards. Just like Atahualpa had been made a prisoner and puppet ruler, Pizarro would be Manco Inca's prisoner and puppet. But in order for this to happen, Quizo would have to successfully take the city. And as he would soon learn that such a thing would not be an easy task, despite all of his previous successes.

If Quizo had the ability to overrule Manco Inca, he could have told him that the mission was doomed to fail. Lima was situated on a flat open plain, which negated all of the advantages that Quizo had previously exploited. He had destroyed the Spaniards by luring them into narrow passes while he had his men stationed up high, allowing them to rain down death on those below.

Now Manco Inca was having him take his best men to charge out into an open flat plain against the Spanish, whose horses, armor, and steel swords made them seem nearly invulnerable to the maces and clubs wielded by Inca foot soldiers. Yet, orders were orders, so Quizo proceeded as Manco Inca directed him. Quizo's army encircled the city and attempted to press in on all sides.

As they approached, Francisco Pizarro gave the order to attack. First, a group of Spaniards wielding guns called harquebusiers opened fire on the huge Inca army, decimating the front line. This was immediately followed by a charge of eighty Spaniards on horseback. They rode right into the smokey aftermath of the gun blasts, wreaking havoc with their swords and pikes.

The Incas attempted to fend off the Spaniards, but predictably enough, their maces were unable to even make a dent in their enemy's armor. After much bloodshed, the Incas were forced to retreat. For a time, they took up the higher ground of the hills that encircled Lima. Quizo must have known how hopeless his situation was, but he decided to roll the dice and told his captains that they would make one final overwhelming charge into the city and that he himself would lead it.

This fateful decision would lead to one of the worst defeats in military history. In the first few moments of this desperate charge, Pizarro again unleashed his cavalry, and they made a beeline straight for Quizo. The horses tore through the front lines of the Incas, and Quizo was rendered into a bloody, trampled corpse. The massive Inca invasion of Lima was over.

Quizo was the glue that held this contingent of Inca warriors together, and when word spread that he was killed in the first round of this renewed spate of fighting, the Incas lost their will to fight and fled from the Spaniards. It took a few days for a runner to reach Manco Inca and inform him of what had happened. One can only imagine the utter despair that he felt upon learning of this terrible upset.

But the plot of this complex drama was about to get much thicker, for the former governor of Cuzco and grizzled conquistador explorer—Diego de Almagro—returned from his expedition south after venturing into the lands that would later become Chile. Almagro learned of what was happening, and to the shock of the Pizarro faction, he sent emissaries to Manco Inca, insisting that he wished to negotiate with the Inca ruler directly.

Diego de Almagro expressed disgust with how the Pizarro brothers had treated him and insisted that he would set things right if Manco Inca met with him. Almagro was indeed on friendly terms with Manco Inca before he left, and his sympathy might have been genuine. But he also had ulterior motives in wishing to side with Manco Inca.

Almagro had come back from Chile empty-handed and realized that the grand Inca capital of Cuzco was likely the best prize he could hope to receive. Wishing to one-up the Pizarros, whom he had long despised, he sought to engineer his own takeover, with Manco Inca as his willing puppet.

Manco Inca initially entertained the notion of aligning himself with Almagro. But ultimately, he decided that none of the Spaniards and their promises could be trusted. Manco Inca was also not willing to go back into a subordinate role. So, he declined the offer. Not only that, when Diego de Almagro and a detachment of his troops sought out Manco Inca's audience, they were greeted by his warriors instead. Almagro was driven off and had to accept that there would not be any grand alliance with the Inca ruler.

Instead, Almagro decided to take on the besieged Hernando Pizarro of Cuzco on his own. On April 8th, 1537, Almagro did what many of his Spanish brothers in arms considered unthinkable—he launched a military coup in Cuzco. He sent his forces to fan out into the city under the darkness of night and take Hernando and his troops by surprise. Diego de Almagro was successful in his takeover and forcibly ripped Cuzco out of Hernando's hands.

Manco Inca took advantage of this distraction to allow himself to slip away. He managed to take a whole army and, in essence, the last remnant of a free and unshackled Inca civilization with him into exile. He took what remained of his army and entourage and relocated farther east to establish a much more remote stronghold in a region the Incas called Antisuyu. Manco Inca stayed here for a time. He remained just out of reach and was a constant thorn in the Spaniards' sides.

Chapter 4 – Last Gasps of Rebellion

"To our Indian eyes, the Spaniards looked as if they were shrouded like corpses. Their faces were covered with wool, leaving only the eyes visible, and the caps that they wore resembled little red pots on top of their heads. Sometimes they also decorated their heads with plumes. Their swords appeared very long, since they had to be carried with the points turned in a backward direction. They were all dressed alike and talked together like brothers and ate at the same table."

-Felipe Guamán Poma de Ayla

While Emperor Manco Inca was establishing himself on the easternmost edges of his former empire, Diego de Almagro was gearing up for an all-out civil war with the Pizarro brothers. The two factions ultimately came to blows on April 26th, 1538. In the swampy terrain of Las Salinas, which was a couple of miles away from Cuzco, the forces of the Pizarro brothers and Diego de Almagro collided. Francisco Pizarro stayed behind in Lima, leaving it up to his battle-hardened brother Hernando to lead the charge against Almagro.

The Spaniards were now not just struggling against the Incas. They were also fighting over which faction of the Spaniards would have control of the former Inca capital. It is said that Diego de Almagro's forces numbered around five hundred, while Hernando's forces were around eight hundred. Hernando obviously had the upper hand, and the fact that Diego de Almagro ended up outnumbered like this sheds some light as to why he might have attempted to get Manco Inca on his side.

If Almagro had the support of a huge army of Inca auxiliaries, he could have taken on the Pizarro faction easily. But Manco Inca refused to get further entangled in the infighting among the Spaniards. Diego de Almagro had come up short and was facing an uphill struggle against his foes.

Hernando's forces used the tried-and-true tactic of starting their attack by firing their noisy and loud harquebus guns prior to launching a cavalry attack. But, of course, instead of charging into mace-wielding Inca troops on the ground, his cavalry was charging into another set of Spanish troops on horseback, their pikes and swords at the ready. It was a titanic struggle, and it wasn't immediately clear who would win.

Prior to the battle, Diego de Almagro made Manco Inca's brother, Paullu Inca, a puppet ruler to create a sense of legitimacy. Paulu had been crowned the previous year in 1537. Almagro had Paullu Inca direct a group of Inca warriors to remain on the fringes of the battle. They were not to actively engage but to stand at the ready to decimate retreating troops. It was arranged so that they could participate in a planned rout of the enemy. Ironically enough, however, when it became clear that Diego de Almagro's forces were the ones retreating, the crafty Paullu Inca immediately turned on his former benefactor and ordered the Inca warriors to attack Almagro's troops instead. Paullu knew full well that it would do him no good to fight a losing battle for Almagro, so he threw in his lot with the Pizarro faction in the hopes that he could gain their favor.

As Diego de Almagro's army was being destroyed, he ran off to Sacsayhuamán, the same fortress that Manco Inca had previously been besieged in just outside of Cuzco. It is hard telling what was in Diego de Almagro's mind besides buying himself a few hours of time. After all, one man could not hold off a whole army for very long.

Almagro eventually surrendered and became Hernando Pizarro's prisoner. He languished in chains for a few months before he was informed that he had been found guilty of treason and was sentenced to death. This death sentence was carried out on July 8th, 1538. Almagro was given his last rites and strangled to death by way of that cruel instrument of death—the garrote.

Meanwhile, Manco Inca set about establishing a new capital in the eastern fringes of his former empire. Deep in the Amazon jungle, his followers cleared out a whole swathe of trees and underbrush, where they built the elegant stone buildings that the Incas were known for. To the wonder of the local Amazonians, who largely lived in the wild, away from any trappings of civilization, Manco Inca's builders quickly reproduced an Inca town square.

The city came complete with stone temples, royal buildings, lodgings, and complex irrigation systems. This new Inca stronghold was called Vilcabamba. Interestingly enough, this new Inca capital soon became a massive trading hub in the region and created a complex network deep in the Amazon wilderness. Inca trading posts routinely exchanged copper-headed Inca maces and axes for the goods the Amazonian tribes had to offer, which ranged from honey and turtle eggs to gold and hardwood building materials.

Along with Manco Inca's trade networks, he also maintained a complex communications network. From this remote corner of the Inca Empire, he was sending messages as far away as Cuzco, where his brother, Paullu Inca, had been placed as a puppet ruler of the Pizarro brothers. He was urging all Incas not to recognize Paullu Inca and to continue actively rebelling against the Spaniards whenever the opportunity arose.

It is important to note that while there were millions of Incas living in Peru, there were still only a couple of thousand Spaniards scattered through certain key cities, such as Lima and Cuzco. It's quite astonishing to think that so few could lord over so many, but this was indeed the situation at the time. However, Spanish control largely ended in the cities. Any attempt to venture out of the cities was always fraught with danger.

The countryside was out of the Spaniards' grasp. If the Incas wished to ambush them as they traveled along an isolated road, they certainly could. This was essentially what Manco Inca was urging them to do. And soon, there were many ambush-styled attacks waged on the Spaniards as they crossed key passes between their strongholds. These attacks were not just waged on armed conquistadors but also on regular merchant trains. The merchants would be killed or taken prisoner, and their goods would be carried off.

These attacks crippled trade between cities. Soon enough, it was realized that fully controlling Peru would be very difficult until Manco Inca, the mastermind behind this slow-burning insurrection, was defeated once and for all. Tasked with this challenge was a Spanish captain by the name of Illán Suárez de Carbajal.

Suárez and a company of two hundred Spanish cavalrymen arrived at the village of Andahuaylas on the fringes of the Amazon. Here, he learned the exact location of Manco Inca's hidden capital from local spies. He immediately set off in that direction and positioned his men just west of Manco Inca's fortified position. Intending to surround Manco Inca and cut off any escape, he sent thirty of his cavalrymen to circle around and position themselves just east of Manco Inca's location. Leading this group of thirty was someone named Captain Villadiego.

Captain Villadiego learned that Manco Inca was in a vulnerable and fairly precarious position at the moment, as he only had eighty warriors to protect him. Typically, due to the advantage of horses and Spanish swords and armor, dispatching such a group would not have been much of a problem. As such, Captain Villadiego, seeking to gain glory for himself, defied his instructions to stay put until directed and charged ahead to take Manco Inca on his own.

As Captain Villadiego made his approach, Manco Inca was alerted and immediately took evasive action. Defenders positioned on high showered the invaders with a barrage of stones. Manco Inca hopped on a Spanish horse, with three other nobles following his lead. With Spanish lances in hand, the four Inca horsemen led a daring charge at the intruders.

The Incas altogether successfully tore into the thirty Spaniards, literally knocking them off-balance. Many of them actually fell to their deaths from the heights in the aftermath. Just imagine a group of armored Spaniards getting knocked over like steel-plated bowling pins and tumbling down the side of the rock face. The results were as deadly as they were dramatic.

Manco Inca and his fellow horse riders had apparently not only learned how to ride a horse on their first try but had also become experts at navigating the treacherous terrain on horseback. Their exploits startled the company of Spaniards.

This daring charge was then followed by a rush of Inca foot soldiers, who finished off the Spaniards who remained. This was a stunning blow for Pizarro, and his distress at what had happened can be seen in a letter dated February 27th, 1539. In this missive, he explains the dire situation he was in to the Spanish king and Holy Roman emperor, Charles V.

Even though he highlights all of the disruptions Manco Inca has caused during his attempts to pacify Peru, Francisco Pizarro ends this note to Charles V vowing that he "will have [Manco] in [his] hands, dead or a prisoner." Although Manco Inca would eventually perish, it would be several years later, and it would not be by way of Francisco Pizarro. At any rate, Pizarro would most certainly remain empty-handed by the end of that summer.

In April 1539, Francisco Pizarro sent his brother Gonzalo to lead a contingent of Spanish troops to hunt down Manco Inca. They made their way through the thick Amazonian jungle until they reached Vilcabamba Valley. They eventually spotted some recently built bridges and attempted to traverse them. These bridges had been built on Manco Inca's orders as part of an elaborate trap. His warriors were lying in wait high up above, with giant boulders at the ready.

As soon as the Spaniards began crossing the bridges, they rolled the boulders down on top of them. The boulders pulverized the front lines of the troops and sent a few Spaniards to their death. However, the trap was sprung a bit too soon. If the Incas had waited until the Spaniards were farther across, the damage would have been much more devastating. As it were, only the front-line troops were hit, and the rest were able to make a hasty retreat.

Nevertheless, Gonzalo and his men were pushed back and had to flee for their lives as Amazonian archers began to open up on them. This rout would cost the Spaniards thirty-six men, which was more than enough to halt their advance. Gonzalo had his men regroup at a fallback position. They would try their luck again several days later. They made their way to the gates of Vilcabamba, where they were confronted with a strange sight: a large stone wall with window-like openings.

They approached it, only to be greeted with explosions and smoke. They soon realized the reason for the barricade. It was being used by Inca warriors armed with stolen Spanish guns! After getting over their fright, the Spaniards were able to rally and storm the barricade again.

Gonzalo had another detachment secretly climb up a back route. This group was able to go around the barrier and surprise the defenders. When Manco Inca figured out that this had been achieved and that his fortress had been compromised and was likely to be overrun, he decided to retreat. He hurriedly fled across a nearby river and once again escaped the Spaniards' grasp.

And as fate would have it, the man who started it all—Francisco Pizarro—would meet his own end before Manco Inca would meet his. On June 26th, 1541, a group of disgruntled former followers of the slain Diego de Almagro stormed into Francisco's home in Lima and assassinated him. The group had long been held at arm's length due to its previous association with the disgraced Almagro, and in their desperation, the men had determined that their only hope of rising up in the hierarchy of Peru would be to kill Francisco Pizarro so that a new governor could be appointed.

The absurdity of this logic is striking since it is hard to fathom how they thought they could be rehabilitated, even under a new governor, after committing such an act. Nevertheless, these brazen men stormed Pizarro's compound, and after a brief struggle with Pizarro and some of his guests, they subdued the old conquistador, stabbing and slashing him several times before someone delivered the killing blow by smashing a vase into Francisco Pizarro's head.

All but one of these assassins would be hunted down and killed by those loyal to the slain Pizarro. The only one to escape this dragnet was a man by the name of Diego Mendez. Mendez had somehow managed to slip away and actually ventured into Manco Inca's territory in Vilcabamba. He and six of his companions (who were not involved in Francisco Pizarro's assignation) made their way through the Amazon jungle to Manco Inca's doorstep.

They pleaded with the Inca ruler for refuge in the one place in Peru where they felt they might be safe. Manco Inca had already heard of how Francisco Pizarro had been killed, and he couldn't help but applaud their effort. Learning that Diego Mendez was one of the assassins was indeed a plus in his book for the Spaniards to stay. Manco Inca finally agreed to shield the assassin and his cohorts, but due to the past double dealings he had experienced with the Spanish, he made sure to put some distance between himself and his new guests.

He had them settle at a place called Vitcos, which was several miles from where he resided. In return for the sanctuary Manco Inca provided, the Spaniards instructed Inca warriors on Spanish military tactics, such as how best to ride a horse into battle and how to use captured Spanish weaponry.

Manco Inca made the fatal mistake of becoming friendly with the strangers and letting his guard down. Since his youth, he had been in the company of these strange foreigners, and despite all of the terrible things that had happened, some part of him must have been genuinely fond of them. He was soon a regular visitor at Vitcos, where he laughed and played games with the Spaniards.

His favorite game to play with them was horseshoes. The game involved tossing a horseshoe toward a pole or stake in the ground, with the goal being to have the horseshoe strike the pole and slide right down the center of it. This classic pastime is still enjoyed in backyards all over the globe, and it was apparently quite entertaining for Manco Inca in Peru hundreds of years ago as well.

However, his love for tossing around the old horseshoe would ultimately do him in. One fine day in 1544, while Manco Inca had his back turned and was getting ready to toss a horseshoe, Diego Mendez and company decided to strike. They leaped upon him and stabbed him several times before slipping away into the wilderness.

But what was the reason for this vicious attack? Diego Mendez had learned that Peru had been given a new viceroy named Don Blasco Nuñez Vela in 1544 (the Viceroyalty of Peru had been established two years prior). And somehow or other, the notion had popped into his warped mind that if he killed the rebel Inca emperor, he and his men would be able to convince the new governor to grant them pardons. Even if such a thing were possible, Diego and his followers would not live long enough to experience it.

The hysterical cries of villagers who had seen the attack sent shockwaves through the whole community, and a large group of warriors was sent to find the killers. They were soon tracked down, and each and every one of the Spaniards was killed.

Manco Inca managed to live long enough to hear that his killers had been killed. His attendants gathered his bloody, battered body and did their best to try and save his life, but it was no use. Just before he perished, he designated an heir: his nine-year-old son Sayri Túpac.

Chapter 5 – Post-Inca Life in Peru

"They seemed like viracochas, which is the name we gave in ancient times to the creator of all things. And they [the Incas] named those people whom they had seen in this way in part because they were very different in clothing and appearance and also because they rode giant animals which had feet of silver, and they said this because of the shining of their horseshoes. They called them viracochas because of their excellent appearance and because of the great differences among them: because some had black beards and others red ones, and because they saw them eat off silver plates, and because they had illapas—our name for thunder—and they said this to describe the harquebuses [guns] because they thought them to be thunder from heaven."

-*Titu Cusi*

After the Spaniards had largely put the Inca Empire to rest, they began to center their efforts on economically developing the region. Much gold and silver had been robbed from the Inca treasury, and the Spaniards knew that there was more where that came from. So, they set about establishing silver mines. A system was subsequently created for tapping the local population for labor. The forced labor of indigenous people in the mines was a grueling and terrible task that often resulted in death.

People died in the mines by way of an instantaneous mine collapse or prolonged exposure to noxious fumes during excavations called "mine sickness." It was a terrible life, and many fled from it, which led to a depopulation of the region. Many natives fled as far as they could from the hated Spanish silver mines of Peru.

Nevertheless, silver and gold continued to be loaded up literally by the boatload and shipped back to Spain. Peru would soon become the biggest money maker of the Spanish American colonies.

However, not everyone turned a blind eye to the suffering of the locals. Complaints were eventually raised with the ruler of Spain, Charles V.

King Charles V apparently was overcome with a stroke of genuine remorse upon hearing reports of these egregious trespasses and set about creating new rules and regulations on how affairs in the Americas should be conducted. These measures were referred to as the New Laws and measures sought to address some of the problems and provide some limited assurances to the local labor pool.

These laws expressly forbade the practice of forced labor, then known as the encomienda system. Word of these reforms came as something of a shock to those who ran the mines since forced labor was their primary means of extracting material from the mines. At first, they attempted to ignore Charles V's ruling, but soon enough, local administrators had to comply. Once it became clear that there would be an impending labor shortage at the mines, Spanish settlers rose up in revolt against the Spanish governor.

The uprising was headed by Francisco Pizarro's brother Gonzalo Pizarro, who led an armed insurrection against Spanish governor Blasco Nuñez Vela in 1544. Gonzalo ended up killing Blasco during the struggle. He demonstrated his utter contempt at the king's measures by placing the former governor's head on a pike for all to see.

While all of this discord was playing out between the two factions in the colonies, neither side was aware that Charles V had already reversed course. It seems King Charles feared losing control of the status quo, which trumped his previous concern for the well-being of the locals. Upon realizing the pushback that the reforms had ignited among the settlers, he had the encomienda system reauthorized once again.

Charles V apparently did not like the encomienda system, but he also did not like the chaos that would erupt if it were removed. So, with a heavy heart, he caved into the demands of the Spanish settlers. Even so, Gonzalo Pizarro and his band were considered outlaws, and nothing could change that fact. One of the first tasks of the new viceroy—Pedro de la Gasca—was to hunt down Gonzalo Pizarro. Gonzalo was finally captured in 1548 and subsequently executed for what he had done.

Spanish explorers used Peru as their base while making inroads farther south, exploring what would one day become modern-day Chile. The Spanish would set down roots there. They felt the remoteness of this strip of land jutting far south and would refer to it as the "End of the Earth." Even today, those who visit certain remote stretches of Chile might agree with these remarks.

Chile's far southern latitudes are much colder than many parts of South America. Sugar and other prized crops could not be grown here. However, wheat crops proved to grow well in this colder climate, suddenly rendering Chile the breadbasket of the region. And Chile would prove to be an important producer of this staple product for Peru and much of the rest of South America.

In 1569, Spain's new king, Philip II (Charles V's son), placed Francisco de Toledo in charge of Peru. The rebel Inca kingdom was ruled by a son of the late Manco Inca—Titu Cusi. Titu Cusi realized that he could not endure a prolonged war with the Spaniards and instead had been playing a long, protracted game with them. While fanning the flames of rebellion in all corners of the former Inca Empire, he kept open diplomatic channels with the Spanish, making it seem as if he were open to reaching some sort of truce or negotiation.

As a part of this ongoing process, in 1569, Titu Cusi agreed to allow two Christian monks—Diego Ortiz and Marcos Garcia—to stay in his kingdom so that they could establish churches. Titu Cusi was not about to give up the faith of his ancestors, but he pragmatically agreed to this intrusion to give himself some diplomatic breathing room with the ever-encroaching Spaniards.

However, the two friars overstayed their welcome, as they began to become a bit too zealous in their preaching for many local Incas' liking. The two priests eventually got mixed up in the destruction of an important Inca shrine. They were blamed for burning it down, although there is no firm proof of who did it. Marcos Garcia apparently was considered most at fault for these trespasses since he was immediately booted out of the kingdom and told not to come back. Diego Ortiz was allowed to stay, but he was severely chastened by the experience. His situation was precarious, but it would become worse in May 1571 when the Inca ruler, Titu Cusi, abruptly perished.

Titu Cusi apparently died of natural causes, but somehow or other, the grieving populace blamed Diego Ortiz. He was apparently nowhere near Titu at the time of his death, but since the priest was viewed as a kind of magical shaman by the people, they were somehow convinced he had put a spell on the king and caused him to die. The stunned Ortiz was seized by an angry mob and brought to the dead emperor. Incredibly enough, the crowd demanded that Ortiz resurrect the Inca king from the dead.

The crowd apparently had been preached to about Christianity enough to know that the main theme of the religion was the resurrection of Jesus Christ and the prophesized resurrection of the dead in the end times. They also likely knew the stories of how Christ and even his followers had supposedly resurrected the dead during his own earthly ministry. The crowd now tried to see if Ortiz could do the same.

Ortiz was a Christian believer, so he wasn't going to deny that such a thing might be possible. And it is said that he did pray fervently for the Inca king to live again. But when it was clear that Titu Cusi was not going to be raised from the dead any time soon, the angry crowd demanded answers from Ortiz. Predictably enough, Ortiz stated that although God could raise anyone from the dead, it simply must not be his will to raise the Inca ruler at this time. The crowd did not like this answer, and Ortiz was immediately seized, beaten, and subjected to all manner of abuse.

In the meantime, Titu Cusi's brother, Túpac Amaru, had been crowned emperor. Ortiz's suffering didn't come to an end until Túpac Amaru ordered his execution. However, Túpac Amaru knew that the killing of a priest gave the Spaniards all the pretext they needed to invade.

He initially sought to keep the whole thing quiet. Soon, though, envoys from the Spaniards began to arrive. The first envoy failed to return, leaving the Spaniards wondering what had happened, so another was sent. Only one man managed to return from this envoy. He was severely injured and relayed an account of how the Incas had attacked his entourage. This led to another envoy being sent, demanding answers from Túpac Amaru. This one, too, was attacked. Viceroy Toledo felt he had all the pretext he needed to launch an invasion of the Inca realm.

In June 1572, he sent out a large army. Initially, the Inca defenders stood up to the Spaniards, but when it was clear they would not be able to prevail, the Incas melted into the landscape and disappeared. The

Spaniards arrived at the capital of Vilcabamba to find it abandoned. They would later learn that the emperor had escaped and was on the run. However, Túpac Amaru was soon cornered, and by September, he was being led to Cuzco in chains. The end of Túpac Amaru and the official resistance of the Inca state would come by way of his execution on September 24th, 1572.

As an interesting aside, the famed 1990s rapper Tupac Shakur was named after Túpac Amaru. His mother was a history buff and wanted to name her son after an influential revolutionary indigenous leader. As a result, most people today probably associate the name Tupac more with rap music than the Inca Empire, but the name did indeed come from the Incas.

Along with being responsible for destroying this last holdout of the Inca Empire, Viceroy Toledo also revamped the old encomienda system of labor to procure as much silver from the mines as he could. Toledo also made sure that Lima was made the center of Peru, overriding the importance of the old Inca capital of Cuzco. Lima would later become the capital of Peru.

So, in this tale of two cities, the once-grand Cuzco deteriorated and became depopulated while the city of Lima grew in wealth and population. Toledo played a large role in this shift in population by resettling many of the native Peruvians, who labored for him in the mines. It is said that under his administration, over a million natives were relocated to new settlements centered around the operation of the mines.

Toledo had three "objectives" in mind during his time as viceroy. One was, of course, the relocation of natives. He also wanted to put a form of routine taxation in place and establish readily available laborers for the mines. The relocation of local populations around the mines was done to achieve all three of these things.

The welfare of these miners who labored to enrich Spain was hardly taken into consideration. As mentioned, the hard labor, abysmal air quality, and the constant threat of collapse were routine risks for anyone forced to labor in the mines.

Due to the deaths in the mines, the deaths from disease, and the migrations from their homelands, the population of the native Peruvians went into a tailspin for much of the 1570s, leading to a dramatic decline. The void that was created allowed Spanish immigrants to spread out and commandeer huge tracts of land. As fortuitous as this might have seemed for the Spaniards, the growing labor shortage presented a huge problem.

The volume of silver and gold extracted from the colony continued to decline and was reaching a problematic level when a massive earthquake rocked Peru in October of 1687, further exacerbating the situation. This earthquake is believed to have reached a magnitude of between 8.4 and 8.7. Such a quake is capable of considerable devastation, and Lima is said to have received the worst of it.

In the aftermath, living conditions in Peru understandably declined. In a bid to improve the economic output of Peru, a series of reforms were put in place known as the Bourbon Reforms, which began to increase taxation. Previously, Peru filled up Spain's coffers through its export of gold and silver, but with this precious resource in decline, it was determined that the deficit would be made up through taxation.

Perhaps most devastating was the enforcement of a sales tax called the alcabala, which greatly disrupted local trade. Taxes are never popular, and their implementation eventually sparked a major rebellion in Peru. Adding to the discontent was a ruling executed in 1776, which partitioned parts of old Peru into what would later become Bolivia and Argentina. The southern section of Peru that was lopped off would become known as Upper Peru and would include all of the vitally important silver mines, such as those found in Potosí, which today stands as a vital resource for modern-day Bolivia.

Yes, just with the stroke of someone's pen in faraway Spain, a huge and vital chunk of Peru was cut away from the vast bulk of local Peruvians. Like the engineering of some sort of financial canal, this move cut off great benefits that had been flowing into Cuzco and Lima and were redirected to the new region of Upper Peru, especially to the growing Spanish settlement of Buenos Aires. The name of this city means "good airs." Yes, after polluting much of Peru with noxious fumes from the mines, the Spaniards themselves were likely seeking a place with "good air."

There was great resentment for these measures, and an all-out revolt soon broke out against them. This rebellion was led by a man of partial Inca descent who called himself Túpac Amaru II. He sought to include not just those of Inca heritage but also all those who were born and raised in Peru in a massive rebellion against Spanish rule.

It is important to note that at this point in Peruvian history, there was a growing population of mestizos. Although the term is considered by some to be highly offensive today, the term mestizo refers to anyone who was born from the union of a Spanish settler and an indigenous native.

Ever since the days of the Spanish Reconquista, when Spaniards struggled to rid the Iberian Peninsula of Islamic invaders, the Spanish had begun creating various categories of people in their society. These categories were initially in reference to religion. It was quite common in the reclaimed lands of Iberia for the Spaniards to refer to Muslim converts to Christianity as Moriscos and Jewish converts as Conversos. These appellations were initially used to distinguish religious status, but they began to be increasingly used to designate different categories of ethnicity as well.

The Spaniards continued this pattern in the New World. Upon their arrival and all throughout the Americas, they would label folks based upon whatever ethnic category they were believed to fall into, creating labels like mestizo and mulatto to try and categorize everyone according to their perceived ancestry. Again, such things are considered highly offensive today, but this was the routine practice of the Spaniards in the New World.

At any rate, Túpac Amaru II, who claimed to be the descendent of the original Inca emperor, was considered a mestizo. He had a large following among both mestizos and indigenous natives, whom he identified with by taking on the mantle of the Inca emperors of old. He also sought to gain support from the creoles, those who were directly descended from European Spaniards but had been born and raised in Peru.

After several decades of worsening conditions in Peru, an all-out rebellion led by Túpac Amaru II erupted. On November 4th, 1780, Túpac led a group of rebels to Tinta in an insurrection, which resulted in the seizure of Spanish administrator Antonio de Arriaga. In a stroke of deceptive brilliance, Túpac Amaru II ordered Antonio to fire off several letters asking for large sums of money and arms.

Túpac Amaru II was essentially tricking the Spanish government into funding his own revolt against them. Shortly after Antonio had fulfilled this task, Túpac Amaru II had the administrator publicly executed in front of a huge group of his cheering followers. After Antonio's death, Túpac Amaru II had "crossed the Rubicon," meaning he had come to a point of no return.

Realizing as much, he gave his followers a lengthy speech in which he highlighted all of the reasons for his decision to rebel against the Spanish authorities. He stressed how he intended to put an end to unfair labor practices and unfair taxation. After giving this speech, Túpac Amaru II began roving about the countryside, gathering an even larger following as he actively recruited from the discontented masses of Peru.

His first major challenge came on November 17th when he and thousands of his supporters came into open conflict with an assembled Spanish army of some six hundred Spanish troops and some seven hundred native auxiliaries. Túpac Amaru II and his followers fought fiercely and ultimately forced the Spanish forces to flee.

Proving that he wasn't above acts of sheer terror, the following day, Túpac Amaru II ordered his troops to destroy a church that had been serving as a shelter for those fleeing from the tumult. Túpac Amaru II then headed farther south, just out of reach of the Spanish authorities. Here, in the southern Peruvian plateau, Túpac Amaru II set up shop and dug in his heels, intending to stay.

That December, Túpac Amaru II and his cohorts launched an ill-fated siege of Cuzco. They were met with heavily fortified Spanish defenders, who had recently been reinforced by fresh troops sent from Lima. Túpac Amaru II and his troops were ultimately pushed back, and they were forced to flee in January of 1781. From here on out, Túpac Amaru II's rebellion began to lose momentum, with many of his previous supporters peeling away from the movement.

Exacerbating this situation was the fact that Spanish authorities announced they would grant amnesty to any of Túpac Amaru II's followers who simply gave up the fight. Túpac Amaru II's increasingly dwindling army was finally cornered by a large Spanish force commandeered by Jose del Valle that March. Túpac Amaru II and his core followers attempted to break out of this encirclement, but he and his whole family were captured and brought into custody on April 6th, 1781.

Túpac Amaru II was ultimately executed on May 18th and in a quite horrific fashion. He was drawn and quartered. This involved tying horses to his arms and legs and having them ride off in opposite directions in an attempt to pull the unlucky Túpac Amaru II apart. The key word here is "attempt." And it turned out to be an attempt for Túpac Amaru II.

Although he was horribly injured, with his arms and legs ripped out of their sockets, he was not pulled apart as intended. The Spaniards, fed up with the delay, ordered their victim, who was writhing in utter agony, to have his head and limbs forcibly cut off.

So, it seemed that the last major revolt of Peru was over, but ironically enough, just a couple of decades later, Peru and just about every other part of Latin America would gain their independence from Spain.

Chapter 6 – Peruvian Independence

"Nations will march toward the apex of their greatness at the same pace as their education. Nations will soar if their education soars; they regress if it regresses. Nations will fall and sink in darkness if education is corrupted or completely abandoned."

- Simón Bolívar

The real key to unlocking Peruvian independence, as well as the independence of many other Latin American countries, came when French dictator Napoleon Bonaparte took over Spain, making the former Spanish monarch, King Ferdinand VII, a prisoner. The French takeover of Spain sent the Spanish colonies into chaos. The inhabitants of Peru suddenly no longer had to answer to the Spanish Crown.

As such, the disruption of the Spanish monarchy in 1808 by the forces of Napoleon Bonaparte created a sense of de facto independence even before any wars of revolution had begun. Peru, however, was a complicated place, and despite the power vacuum that had been created by the severing of the Spanish Crown, there were two distinct factions in place. There was a faction that vied for complete and utter independence, and there was a faction that voiced support for the monarchy.

As such, a struggle would ensue that would not come to a close until 1824. This time around, the revolutionaries were not led by those claiming Inca descent but rather by two wealthy Spanish-descended settlers: Simón Bolívar, who came from what would eventually become Venezuela, and José de San Martín, who hailed from what we now call Argentina. These two led a massive revolt in 1819. They even had warships that were lent by Chile, which were used to secure the Pacific coast.

José de San Martín is an interesting character in his own right. Although he was born in Argentina, he studied abroad in Spain as a young man. While he was in Spain, he became involved in the Peninsular War, where Spanish patriots attempted to eject the French invaders. It is somewhat ironic that this veteran of the Peninsular War would then return to his home in Argentina to take up arms against the Spanish Crown!

However, such things are no more ironic than revolutionary George Washington fighting for the British during the tumult of the French and Indian War and then going on to kick the British out of the colonies. History is full of all kinds of ironies and reversals of fortune.

Simón Bolívar came from a similar background as José de San Martín. Just like San Martín, he was born to a prominent family of Spanish descent, and just like San Martín, he was born in the New World. Also, like José de San Martín, Simón Bolívar was educated in Spain as a young man.

Simón Bolívar.
https://commons.wikimedia.org/wiki/File:Sim%C3%B3n_Bol%C3%ADvar,_Toro_Moreno,_Jos%C3%A9,_1922,_Legislative_Palace,_La_Paz.png

In the mother country of Spain, this man of Spanish descent read about the ideals of the growing intellectual movement afoot in Europe known as the Enlightenment. The ideals of this movement convinced

Bolívar that it was time for the nations of the New World to shake off the shackles of the Old World and gain their independence.

Under the aegis of Simón Bolívar and José de San Martín, several notable battles would follow, such as the Battle of Bombona and the Battle of Pichincha. Simón Bolívar led the charge in the Battle of Junín in August of 1824. The Battle of Junín was critical for the future of Lima since it had been seized by the royalists and had become a stronghold of the opposition.

However, the matter was not settled until after the Battle of Ayacucho. It was here that Peru's independence was truly won. This battle pitted thousands of rebels against the royalists to determine the fate of southern Peru, which was still under the control of the Spanish Crown at the time. The battle was waged on December 9th, 1824, near the town of Ayacucho.

The forces of independence managed to secure a decisive victory. After the battle was won, the question of who would govern the newly independent Peru arose. Simón Bolívar had already been nominated as dictator of the Peruvian nation back in early 1824. This was done by the Congress of Peru, which also created the nation of Bolivia out of Upper Peru, naming it in honor of the hero of the revolution. At this point in Bolívar's illustrious career, he was the head of several South American countries. He was even in charge of Peru and what was then termed Gran Colombia at the same time.

Battle of Ayacucho by *Martín Tovar y Tovar*.
https://commons.wikimedia.org/wiki/File:Batalla_de_Ayacucho_by_Mart%C3%ADn_Tovar_y_Tovar_(1827_-_1902).jpg

Although Peru was independent, it was in a precarious state. It was essentially under martial law, with Bolívar at the helm. Interestingly, even though official independence had been declared in 1824, an enclave of monarch-supporting royalists, located in that same aforementioned Ayacucho, would continue to duke it out and wouldn't be completely disbanded until 1839.

As mentioned, Bolívar was made dictator in January 1824 and was then officially elected president in February 1824. In 1826, Simón Bolívar instituted a new constitution for Peru. He did this in collaboration with Peru's Constituent Assembly, and the final draft was made official by way of Peru's electoral college on December 8th, 1826. The Constitution proved to be highly unpopular and did not sit well with laws that were already on the books.

At this point, both Simón Bolívar and his policies had fallen flat with the people of Peru. Despite Bolívar's previous attraction as a charismatic, dashing revolutionary hero, he was increasingly viewed as an authoritarian tyrant. After Simón Bolívar's term came to a close in 1827, he was replaced by José de La Mar as president of Peru on August 22nd, 1827.

The situation in what used to be known as Upper Peru, which subsequently became known as Bolivia, was quite complicated at this time. There was much tension between Peru and the surrounding regions that were considered to be "Bolivarian" or "pro-Bolívar" in their makeup. Tensions were so high that the Peruvians decided to conduct a preemptive strike of sorts against Bolivia.

This invasion was essentially an effort to install a puppet government that would be friendly to Peruvian interests, and it was successful in that aim. But the invasion of Bolivia, in turn, sparked conflict between Peru and Colombia, which had supported the previous Bolivian regime. Colombia was known as Gran Colombia then, and it was a much larger country than it is today. Gran Colombia consisted of all of modern-day Colombia, Ecuador, Panama, Venezuela, part of Brazil, and parts of modern-day Peru. It was Bolívar's dream to create a grand confederation of states, but the post-Bolívar leadership of Peru did not agree with this goal.

Simón Bolívar had his headquarters in Gran Colombia, and he saw what was happening. He decided to take decisive action by declaring war on Peru. The first battle fought between the two sides—the Battle of

Punta Malpelo—took place on August 31st, 1828. This exchange was a naval battle and resulted in defeat for Gran Colombia. A further blow to the naval forces of the Colombians occurred when Peru successfully put a blockade in place that was able to keep Colombian ships literally at bay. This development ensured that the rest of the war would be fought on land, not at sea.

The drama between Peru and Colombia only came to a close after the decisive Battle of Tarqui on February 27th, 1829, in which the forces of Peru trounced those of Colombia. Gran Colombia soon disintegrated in 1831. Bolivia would maintain its independence as it ushered in the ten-year rule of Bolivian President Andrés de Santa Cruz y Calahumana in 1829.

However, even with Colombia out of the way, there was more trouble in store for Peru when the country was rocked by an all-out civil war in the year 1834. The Peruvian Civil War erupted in 1834 in the aftermath of an election that saw General Luis José de Orbegoso become the nation's provisional president. The results upset his predecessor, General Agustín Gamarra, who encouraged General Pedro Bermúdez to lead a revolt against the Orbegoso government.

Things got out of hand rather rapidly, and Peru was soon split between those who supported Orbegoso (the Obregosistas) and those who supported Bermúdez (Bermudistas). Skirmishes were exchanged back and forth between the two sides over the next few months until a truce was called by way of the Embrace of Maquinhuayo, thereby ending the first civil war in the history of the Peruvian Republic. The end result of this conflict was the recognition of the Orbegoso government and Gamarra fleeing to Bolivia in exile.

A couple of years after this disturbance, in 1836, Peru entered into an agreement with Bolivia called the Peru-Bolivian Confederation. The confederation sought to put the genie back in the bottle as it pertains to pre-partition Peru. It lumped Bolivia back into the Peruvian fold by creating the categories of "North Peru," "South Peru," and, of course, "Bolivia" and placing them into one roughly integrated confederation. This confederation even called for a new capital, with the Peruvian town of Tacna earning that honor. Those who lived in the previous capital of Lima did not care much for this arrangement.

The head of this assortment of Peruvian states was Andrés de Santa Cruz, who was given the somewhat strange-sounding title of "Supreme

Protector."

Shortly after the confederation was established, Chile and Argentina declared war against it. This conflict was known as, what else, the War of the Confederation.

In 1838, with a string of naval victories under their belt, the Chileans began to gain the upper hand. However, the truly decisive moment came during the Battle of Portada de Guías, in which the Chilean forces laid siege to the Peruvian capital of Lima. The city was occupied by enemy forces until August 21st, 1838, when the Chileans abruptly departed upon receiving word that a huge Bolivian army was on its way. The war continued to shift back and forth with no clear winner until the conflict finally came to an end in 1839 at the Battle of Yungay.

This battle was a decisive one, and the confederation forces were finally defeated. The confederation disbanded, and Peru and Bolivia reverted back to their pre-confederation states.

In the meantime, Peru managed to find a lucrative means of supporting itself. Even though the lion's share of the gold and silver had already been taken, Peruvians discovered a new treasure that could really rake in revenue. They discovered the power of a little something called guano.

Guano, which is a form of seabird and bat dung, can be used as a form of fertilizer and is very useful for farming. The guano gleaned from the Peruvian coast is so fertile because it is rich in nitrates from deposits of fecal matter that had largely been left untouched. Due to the environmental conditions of the region, these piles of bird poop had literally piled up and been left relatively undisturbed. And like a finely fermented wine, the guano, over time, became incredibly rich in nitrogen. These nitrates can truly give crops a boost, facilitating faster and more abundant growth. It's for this reason that Peruvian guano became such a hot commodity for farmers.

The product grew in demand, and since Peru's coasts were literally covered in the stuff, it was soon realized that Peru had found a new lucrative product to export far and wide. Peru would dominate the fertilizer market from the 1840s until the 1870s.

Known as the "Guano era," it's said that by the 1860s, Peru was regularly taking in as much as twenty million from its guano exports. Spain apparently took note of this fact and suddenly wanted in on the action. It even went as far as to launch a brief military operation over the fate of a guano-rich island off Peru's coast.

Spanish troops landed on the Chincha Islands and attempted to occupy them until a coalition of Latin American states kicked them out. The Spaniards were driven off, but the incident served as a demonstration of not only how important bird poop had become but also of how vulnerable the status quo of Latin America could be.

At any rate, Peru's dominance in the guano market was only disrupted by a renewed outbreak of war.

Chapter 7 – The War of the Pacific and the Modernization of Peru

"The continuation of authority has frequently proved the undoing of democratic governments. Repeated elections are essential to the system of popular governments, because there is nothing so dangerous as to suffer power to be vested for a long time in one citizen. The people become accustomed to obeying him, and he becomes accustomed to commanding, hence the origin of usurpation and tyranny."

-*Simón Bolívar*

By the 1870s, Peru was making some major strides economically. It had built up a lucrative trade in guano and had been able to engage in massive infrastructure projects. Most notable of all was Peru's bid to build railroads. One of the biggest of these projects involved an American businessman by the name of Henry Meiggs. He was tapped to construct a set of tracks that ran from the coastal town of Callao all the way through the Andes, deep into the interior of the country. The track travels through rough and rugged terrain, and some sections are said to reach an elevation as high as fifteen thousand feet. Known as the Peruvian Central Railway, this railroad is listed as a World Heritage Site and is still in operation to this day.

It was amid this backdrop of relative prosperity and industry that Manuel Pardo came to prominence and was elected as the first so-called "civilian president" of Peru. For many, after a steady stream of generals and other military-affiliated leaders, Pardo, a civilian businessman, was like a breath of fresh air. Pardo had become rich off of guano and knew the value that it could bring. He also knew that Peru risked lagging behind in infrastructure, so he sought to tap into Peru's guano resources and divert the proceeds from them to continuing major infrastructure projects, such as the railroad.

However, Pardo is perhaps best known for establishing the Treaty of Defensive Alliance with neighboring Bolivia in 1873. This treaty was put in place to offset a growing fear of Chilean power in the region. The measure was not popular with everyone (the Chileans, in particular, were deeply concerned about what this treaty meant for them), and Pardo would be assassinated a few years later on November 16th, 1878.

Pardo's fears of a war with Chile would eventually come true. In 1879, Peru and Chile decided they would go to war. However, the war was actually initiated after Bolivia entered into conflicts with Chile and demanded that Peru fulfill its part of the bargain in the Treaty of Defensive Alliance.

The trouble began after the Bolivian government decided to engage in excessive taxation of a Chilean/British mining firm located in Antofagasta. Bolivian leader Hilarión Daza had previously made an agreement with the Chilean government that saw Chile cede part of the Atacama Desert to Bolivia in return for assurance that Bolivia would not raise taxes on Chilean mining outfits in the region. Nevertheless, when the mining company didn't pay up, it was shut down, and its manager was arrested.

The Chilean government sent its troops and settlers back into the region of the Atacama Desert that had been ceded to Bolivia. Daza viewed this as an act of aggression and moved Bolivia to a war footing with Chile. The Chileans showed just how serious they were by conducting naval campaigns against Antofagasta.

It's important to note that due to Chile's connection to Britain, the nation was able to acquire a fairly modern naval force, with its main ships, the *Blanco Encalada* and the *Almirante Cochrane*, being constructed in Hull, England, in 1874.

Peru initially dragged its feet and tried to establish high-level diplomatic talks in an effort to diffuse the crisis but to no avail. On March 14th, 1879, Bolivia officially declared war, and on April 6th, 1879, Chile made its official declaration of war against Bolivia and Peru. The following day, Peru returned the favor and declared war as well.

It was a short time later that Chile managed to use its powerful navy to attempt to shut down Peru's port of Iquique. This led to the Battle of Iquique, which was fought between Chilean and Peruvian navies on May 21st, 1879. The Peruvians proved themselves to be ferocious sailors during the exchange. Most notably, the battleship *Huáscar*—named after the Inca ruler of the same name—rammed the Chilean ship *Esmeralda* and sent it sinking to the bottom of the ocean. The ship was captained by a man named Miguel Grau, who would become a Peruvian national hero before it was all said and done.

Despite the Peruvians' efforts, the more modern, better-armed Chilean fleet won the day. The two navies had a rematch that October in the Battle of Angamos. Here, the Chileans were able to further decimate the Peruvian navy, and the steadfast captain at the helm, Miguel Grau, was killed in action.

On land, battles were waged from Tarapacá, which was part of Peru at the time, to Lima and many points in between. One of the most important battles—the Battle of Tacna—was waged in 1880. This battle resulted in a Chilean victory and the disbanding of the alliance between Bolivia and Peru.

The war ended with the Treaty of Ancón, which was officially recognized by both Peru and Chile on October 20th, 1883. Eventually, it was decided that Chile would be given control of Tarapaca, and Bolivia would enter into new financial agreements with Chilean firms with the promise not to raise taxes.

The greatest blow to Peruvian esteem was the loss of its southern provinces of Tacna and Arica, which were occupied by Chilean forces during the war. Chile was supposed to return the provinces after ten years but clung to them for much longer. The provinces were subjected to the process of "Chilenization." Needless to say, the aftermath of the War of the Pacific left many in Peru understandably unhappy.

A look at the territorial concessions of the Treaty of Ancón.
Janitoalevic, CC BY-SA 4.0 <https://creativecommons.org/licenses/by-sa/4.0>, via Wikimedia Commons https://commons.wikimedia.org/wiki/File:Treaty_of_Anc%C3%B3n.svg

And this bubbling brew of Peruvian discontent would cause another civil war to erupt in 1884. In this conflict, one faction was led by Miguel Iglesias, who had been handpicked by the Chilean occupation, while the other was headed by Andrés Avelino Cáceres, a heroic figure from the War of the Pacific. When the civil war erupted, both Bolivia and Chile weighed in, with the Bolivians supporting the so-called "Caceristas" and Chile supporting the "Iglesistas." The Caceristas ultimately prevailed, and Iglesias was temporarily exiled to Spain before making his fateful return in 1895.

Interestingly, after everything that had happened, Iglesias was quite peaceful. He didn't return to start a war but to run for the Senate. He was elected as a representative for Cajamarca.

Nicolás de Piérola, a critic of Andrés Avelino Cáceres and the military establishment, was then elected president of Peru. Piérola is notable because he was the first president to truly take Peru into a more civilian-oriented administration. He focused on domestic concerns, such as civil freedoms, industrial development, and religious freedom.

During Piérola's time in office, in consideration of all of the literal damage that had been done from the recent military actions, Piérola made rebuilding the infrastructure of Peru his topmost priority. He also sought to reform Peru's economic sector. Piérola's presidency ushered in a time in Peruvian history that would become known as the Aristocratic Republic since the leaders during this time were from aristocratic, elite backgrounds rather than military backgrounds, which had largely been the case in the past.

Peru became increasingly dependent on both British and American businesses to stimulate its own economy. Rubber, in particular, became a big draw in Peru during this time, leading to the Amazon rubber boom. But Peru's industrialization remained slow, as it fell into the trap of being primarily an export economy. Peru exported a few choice products naturally extracted from the region to rake in revenue, but it was forced to import all other modern necessities.

Any country that falls into this trap becomes quite dependent on other nations to keep up with basic infrastructure and obtain modern goods and services. There was also very little in the way of workers' rights for those who toiled away in all of those rubber and other factories in Peru. These facilities resulted in a largely indigenous Peruvian labor pool being routinely exploited.

Because of these circumstances, fresh revolts began to take place, such as the 1896 separatist movement in the region of Loreto, which resulted in a temporary secession from Peru until the troops were called in and broke the insurrectionists up. Just a couple of years later, another round of revolts occurred, and the so-called "Jungle Republic" was established. Once again, the troops had to be sent in, and the ill-fated Jungle Republic was nixed in the year 1900.

After Peru gained independence, it was in a state of turmoil and unrest that was only eased by occasional financial booms, such as the rubber boom and the guano boom. However, if anyone was hoping that the dawning of the 20th century would be a time of relative peace and harmony in comparison, they would be gravely mistaken.

Chapter 8 – The Dawning of a New Century

"It is not possible to democratize the education of a country without democratizing its economy and without democratizing, therefore—its political superstructure."

-José Carlos Mariátegui

As the 20th century dawned, Peru was firmly entrenched as an export economy, and the United States was increasingly becoming its number one patron. Of particular interest to US industrialists at this time was Peru's copper. Copper was and is still used for a wide variety of important aspects of industrialization. Copper is a very conducive material, so it is often used in electronics.

Back then, copper was in demand for radios and telephone equipment. US industrialists were soon actively involved in Peru's mining operations, overseeing the huge labor forces required to extract large amounts of ore. Two transplanted American companies in particular—the Cerro de Pasco Mining Company and the Anaconda Company—took the lead in procuring Peru's copper.

The Peruvian government is said to have been either unwilling or unable to ensure that its workers were not mistreated by ruthless company bosses seeking to turn as much profit as possible. As one might expect, this was a recipe for terrible working conditions in the Peruvian mines. It also created some fairly terrible conditions for the environment.

In 1922, a huge smelter was put up by Cerro de Pasco in the La Oroya district (in Peru's Yauli Province), which resulted in terrible pollution. The land was greatly disturbed by the wanton spilling of hazardous materials, including lead, zinc, sulfur, and even arsenic. As it turns out, Cerro de Pasco failed to install a pollution filter, which went against regulations. As a result, toxic sludge had poured into the landscape, making about half a million acres of what would have otherwise been good farmland absolutely worthless.

Interestingly enough, Cerro de Pasco ended up buying this ruined land at a greatly discounted price. The people down at Cerro de Pasco then installed the needed filters, and once the surrounding land was cleaned up, they proceeded to raise cattle for their own benefit. Since Cerro de Pasco had just bought up over 400,000 acres of land, it became the largest landholder in all of Peru.

One of the most notorious companies to flout labor norms was the Peruvian Amazon Company, founded by Peruvian businessman Julio César Arana del Águila. The company was so harsh on its indigenous workers that it sparked widespread criticism not just in Peru but also around the globe.

Rubber production in Peru is said to have peaked in 1912. After that point, the Far East became the world's biggest rubber producer during the lead-up to World War One.

World War One proved to be very disruptive for Peru's markets, even though Peru chose not to take an active combat role. The native labor pool, in particular, was greatly impacted. All of this set the stage for activists in Peru to finally demand some workers' rights, and interest in the development of some of Peru's first trade unions began in earnest.

There were calls for basic rights, such as an eight-hour workday. It took some demonstrations and loud calls for reform (one of the loudest was the Lima general strike that occurred in May 1919), but basic measures were grudgingly instituted. As is often the case, this heavy emphasis on unionization and basic benefits gave rise to an undercurrent of socialism in Peruvian politics. Those who wanted to uplift the poor and ignored masses saw socialism as a vehicle through which such things could be achieved.

In September 1928, the Socialist Party of Peru was formed. The party was spearheaded by José Carlos Mariátegui. Although ostensibly labeled as socialist, Mariátegui was a diehard communist. The groundwork for

Peruvian communism had already been laid back in 1924 with the creation of the American Popular Revolutionary Alliance or APRA, of which Mariátegui had been a part.

Although it might be common sense for some, there is much confusion in regard to what American means. So, the term "American" in the APRA acronym needs to be addressed. American, in this case, is not in reference to the United States; rather, it means American as in the Americas. The reason people from the United States are often referred to as Americans is because they don't have a better name like Peruvians or Mexicans, for instance. No one wants to call them "Staters" or "US-ers." Although it was likely a lofty goal of some in APRA to have their ideology take root in the United States of America, this would not be the case. APRA was a fairly localized phenomenon unique to Latin America.

At any rate, the organization known as APRA attempted to lay the groundwork for open communist sympathies in Peru. It was from these early seeds that the official Communist Party of Peru would come into being in 1930.

That August, the Great Depression sparked by the New York stock market crash of 1929 finally reached Peru. The summer of 1930 was a rough and uncertain period for Peru, and it was against this backdrop of financial uncertainty that Peruvian Augusto Leguía made his move.

Augusto came to power as dictator of Peru in 1919 and ended the Aristocratic Republic. In its place was the Oncenium of Leguía. This is in reference to the start of the eleven-year rule (Oncenium means eleven) of Peruvian politician Augusto B. Leguía. Leguía would serve as president of Peru from 1919 to 1930.

Leguía's eleven-year run of Peru was known as a more liberal phase in Peruvian governance that featured better civil guarantees. President Leguía sought to improve the healthcare system of Peru and its domestic infrastructure. At the same time, however, Leguía administered Peru in an authoritarian manner and was quick to stifle any opposition to his rule. President Leguía would end up exiling many of his opponents.

The Oncenium would come crashing to an end in 1930 in light of the impending financial collapse. Banks in Peru began to fail, as sales of previously lucrative exports, such as cotton, wool, and copper, dropped by 70 percent. For an export economy dependent upon the sale of its commodities, this was an absolutely dire situation to be in.

Peru needed to stay afloat by selling its wares, yet in light of the Great Depression, the nations of the world just weren't buying like they used to. After several districts of Peru made it known they would not support the military dictator, Lieutenant Colonel Luis Miguel Sánchez Cerro staged a military coup against Leguía on August 24th, 1930. The former Peruvian president (who often behaved more like a dictator) would perish in custody in February 1932.

Cerro in 1920.
https://commons.wikimedia.org/wiki/File:S%C3%A1nchez_Cerro.jpg

There was a backlash against Peruvian communists, and many APRA members were killed or thrown in prison. And amidst this infighting, World War Two erupted in 1939, and Peru suddenly found itself being forced to pick sides. Since their number one benefactor was the United States, it was pretty clear to Peruvian authorities which horse they should bet on.

As such, Peru cut ties with the Axis nations of Italy, Japan, and Germany and began contributing to the Allied cause. These contributions were fairly minor in scope, but Peru tried to do its part all the same. For one thing, Peru was tasked with keeping a close watch on the Panama Canal in case any enemy forces attempted to infiltrate the Western Hemisphere. Peru was also sure to readily supply Allied forces with all of the copper, iron, cotton, and sugar they needed.

Perhaps more controversially, Peru kept a close watch on its Italian, German, and Japanese immigrants since it was possible they were spies for the Axis. These sentiments, which happened in many other parts of the world, created tragic situations in which honest, law-abiding immigrants were targeted. But the situation was a complicated one, and some in the immigrant community did support the fascists of Italy, the Nazis of Germany, and the militarists of Japan.

In fact, some in the immigrant Japanese community in Lima established a large donation fund in 1938 to contribute to the Japanese war effort in China. It is indeed troubling to think that while terrible events like the Rape of Nanking were being perpetuated in China by Japan, there were Japanese immigrants in Peru raising money to help fund the Japanese military machine.

Obviously, such things had to stop. After the United States declared war on Japan in 1941, Peru made it clear that such fundraising schemes would no longer be tolerated. Harsh measures were taken, and in some cases, blatant discrimination against the Japanese community in Peru occurred, with hundreds being deported to the US to live in internment camps. Interestingly enough, it was later learned after the war that Japan had planned to use agents in Peru to sabotage the war efforts but reconsidered after noting the "hostile atmosphere." However, most Japanese in Peru were not agents working for the Japanese government.

One side effect of the war was the development of Peru as an exporter of fish. This came largely as a consequence of Japanese seafood no longer being on the global market. Peru stepped into this void to become a substantial provider of fish in the Pacific. After the Allies successfully concluded World War Two in 1945, Peru began to turn inward again and sort itself out.

There were new calls for democracy and freedom. This makes sense. After all, Peru had helped aid the cause for freedom in World War Two. So, how long until the people of Peru could enjoy a little freedom of their own? These were the questions that many post-war Peruvians couldn't help but ask themselves. Their dreams would largely be crushed when another military coup rocked Peru in 1948.

General Manuel A. Odría used military might to take over the Peruvian government. This was done under the pretense of preventing communist organizers from APRA from organizing a coup of their own. But even though this was a military takeover, Manuel was a populist at heart, and he at least tried to pay lip service to the genuine grievances of the average Peruvian on the street.

General Odría promised the people that military rule would be temporary and that open and fair elections would soon be held. But these promises would prove to be entirely empty.

Chapter 9 – From Military Dictatorship to Modern Peru

"Up to now we have faced external problems in an isolated fashion. One of these problems is precisely the drug trade and what ash been the result? A very weak and fragile position."

-Alberto Fujimori

Upon seizing power, one of the first things the new Peruvian leader, General Odría, did was outlaw communism. Communism was made officially illegal on November 2nd, 1949. Odría then did what he could to ingratiate himself with the two aspects of Peruvian society that mattered to him and his own personal ambition the most. These were the ranks of the military and the ranks of the common people.

Knowing all too well the importance of having solid military backing, General Odría sought to buy the support of the Peruvian Armed Forces by instituting impressive wage increases to the military. And as for the common Peruvian on the street? Odría made sure to enact many of the beneficial social programs that activists had long been calling for to try and help uplift the poor. Although these programs were widely popular with the masses, Peru would virtually bankrupt itself trying to pay for them.

General Odría was clearly playing for keeps, but he would still hold elections. They just wouldn't be fair elections. In the summer of 1950, Odría held what has been widely reported as a rigged election, as he controlled just about every part of the election process. He was even able to trump up phony charges on his main political rival and have him arrested just prior to the election!

His political opponent, another Peruvian general, Ernesto Montagne Markholz, was a long-time critic of General Odría. He was released two weeks after being arrested. But even so, it was made sure that he would no longer be able to mount any political opposition. Ernesto was ultimately deported to Argentina and more than likely told not to run for office against Odría ever again.

With the field cleared of any real opponents, Odría won the election that July. His term was meant to last six years, and by the time those six years were coming to a close, Odría was once again on the ballot, ready and waiting for what he likely believed to be some rather predictable results for the 1956 election. However, one thing made this election unique: the fact that it was the first time that Peruvian women were allowed to take part in it. It's estimated that more than 1.25 million women participated in this election.

A new political force rose through the ranks of Peru's political echelon in an attempt to unseat Odría. This Peruvian political dynamo was named Fernando Belaúnde Terry. But before he could even attempt to challenge Odría for office, his candidacy was denied him. Terry had gone through all of the official channels to begin the process of running, only to have his application rejected.

Terry would go on to become an unofficial opposition leader and lead demonstrations all throughout Peru, decrying what was seen as corrupt electoral practices.

Those who feared Odría would never leave office were shocked when he stepped aside for his hand-picked successor, Manuel Prado Ugarteche, to take over. This was a setback for Fernando Belaúnde Terry, but he wasn't willing to give up. On the contrary, he ran once again in the 1962 election. These elections would be widely viewed as fraudulent. The average Peruvian applauded when the military again stepped in, this time to get rid of President Manuel Prado Ugarteche and put in place a temporary government until new elections could be held the following year.

In 1963, with the threat of electoral malfeasance at bay, Fernando Belaúnde Terry was finally successful at the ballot box. The early 1960s were a tumultuous time for Latin American politics as a whole. The Cuban Revolution had sent shockwaves far and wide. And by 1965, some of these waves had reached Peru in the form of a series of revolutionary movements.

Most notable among them was the Movimiento de Izquierda Revolucionaria, or MIR for short. It was Terry's bad luck to come into office just as things were starting to get stirred up. MIR was headed by a man with roots in APRA: Luis de la Puente Uceda. Uceda and his MIR guerilla fighters spread terror throughout Peru until their remote base located in the vicinity of the Mesa Pelada was bombed to smithereens by the Peruvian Air Force.

With the Peruvian military seemingly unstoppable, Terry was removed from office in yet another military coup that took place in 1968. This moment is viewed as the start of the first phase of the nationalist programs. This latest military coup was executed by General Juan Velasco Alvarado. Although he was known as President Alvarado, he acted more like a dictator. His most pressing concern was how to solve one of Peru's most pressing problems—agrarian reform.

The main problem was that only a few people had land. This situation stemmed back to the Spanish colonial takeover of Peru. President Alvarado sought to fix these problems with the stroke of a pen by forcefully redistributing Peru's land.

Along with kickstarting this aggressive agrarian reform, President Alvarado also made sure to nationalize all of Peru's most productive industries, as well as a few key banking institutions. Nationalization might seem like a good idea, but it only works well when these assets are managed well. And under Alvarado's administration, corruption often took place. His critics felt that Peru suffered more from mismanagement at the top than anything else.

Nevertheless, the old-general-turned-president would cling to power until he was ousted in 1975 by way of a military coup. Alvarado was then replaced by the leader of the coup, General Francisco Morales Bermúdez Cerruti. It was a military dictatorship, but Cerruti would allow a return to free and fair elections in 1980.

In the meantime, agrarian reform was really picking up steam. It is estimated that between 1969 and 1979, some 15,826 pieces of property were forcefully redistributed to around 370,000 beneficiaries, involving a total of over 23 million acres of Peruvian soil.

The completion of this vast agrarian project set the stage for the return of Fernando Belaúnde Terry, who was elected once again as president in May 1980. Many were hopeful for the future, believing that prosperity might be around the corner. But the 1980s was a decade of cocaine and crack, and Peru would be deeply affected by the out-of-control narcotics trade.

Peru's natural environment was an ideal place for remote cocaine factories to begin dotting the rugged landscape. These operations were clandestine, but only to a point. Many of them were hiding in plain sight, shielded by corrupt Peruvian officials. All one has to do is consider the saga of Pablo Escobar in neighboring Colombia, and they get an idea of the kind of corrupt collaboration government officials in Peru had with these drug cartels.

However, the narcotics trade, as can be expected, negatively impacted Peru. Besides feeding a global addiction, the money gleaned from cocaine was often used to fund armed groups. This led to an explosion of armed drug cartels and bands of guerrilla fighters, such as the Túpac Amaru Revolutionary Movement (MRTA) and Shining Path.

Although MRTA took the name of a great rebel leader of the past, this group had more in common with Karl Marx than the Incas. MRTA was an unabashedly Marxist group dedicated to overthrowing the Peruvian government.

However, the terrorist outfit Shining Path would truly take center stage as it pertains to anti-government activities. Shortly after the May 1980 election, Shining Path (known as Sendero Luminoso in Spanish) began to run riot throughout Peru because they were upset with the election results.

A Shining Path poster promoting an electoral boycott.
https://commons.wikimedia.org/wiki/File:Shining_Path_electoral_boycott_poster.jpg

The initial outburst was easily put down, but throughout the 1980s, Shining Path's membership surged. Shining Path became known among the poor people of the Andes Mountains as a kind of vigilante group that stood up for the rights of commoners. Shining Path would become notorious for apprehending anyone whom they felt was guilty of one form of oppression or another, putting them on trial, and summarily executing them.

With these actions, Shining Path was trying to assert itself as the law and authority of Peru—essentially a government within a government. The actual government of Peru, no matter how corrupt it had become due to bribes and fixed elections, could not stomach such a thing, so action had to be taken. However, President Fernando Belaúnde Terry was leery of all of the past military coups and military governments, so he was hesitant to execute an outright military operation.

Nevertheless, in 1981, as the situation continued to deteriorate, he declared martial law in the Andes. The troops were indeed sent in to apprehend members of Shining Path. This was where things got really ugly. The military sought to crush Shining Path and killed many civilians in the process. The methods used by the government were extremely careless and lacked restraint. Just imagine government agents storming an apartment complex and spraying the place with bullets, and you get the idea. Whether it was intentional or not, a lot of civilians died because of their actions. This, of course, only increased support for the militant group. Even though Shining Path was under extreme pressure, it increased its own terrorist activities by targeting the family members of the police and military personnel sent after them.

This was the main problem of putting down a group like Shining Path. Its members were so entangled in the social fabric of Peru that they could easily strike out against not only those who were against them but also their family members. Because of this, the military and police began to wear ski masks just to ensure that their families would not be hurt.

So, this was the state of Peru for much of the 1980s—a war zone involving two armies, one working for the official government and the other for an underground paramilitary group of guerrilla fighters. However, both groups had to cover their faces and live in the shadows.

One of the worst spates of violence from Shining Path occurred in 1983 when they attacked Lima itself. In a highly organized campaign, Lima's main power plant was shut down, sending the city into darkness before a series of pre-planned bombs were set off, rocking the capital. Countless people were killed before it was all said and done.

There would be a changing of the guard in Peru with the election of Alan Garciá to the presidency in 1985. During his administration, Shining Path was largely suppressed, but terrorist attacks from them and other guerilla groups continued. This was something that Alberto Fujimori, upon his election in 1990, promised to stop. Fujimori authorized the Peruvian military to go at the terrorists with both barrels blazing, but they took things a bit too far. On November 3rd, 1991, the army became embroiled in a tragedy known as the Barrios Altos massacre, which left fifteen people dead, one of them an eight-year-old child.

This would generate considerable criticism of both the Peruvian military and Alberto Fujimori. Fujimori had apparently become a law unto himself, and on April 5th, 1992, he launched a kind of internal coup in which he had Congress disbanded. With no congressional check on his authority, things could go as he pleased, and things would get even worse. On July 18th, 1992, another massacre was executed by the Peruvian Armed Forces. At Lima's La Cantuta University, a professor and nine students, who were suspected of having links to Shining Path, were apprehended, tortured, and killed.

A resurgent MRTA stole the headlines in December 1996 when they seized control of the Japanese Embassy in Lima, taking everyone inside hostage. Needless to say, this was really bad press for Peru. It seemed as if the Peruvian government could not even provide basic security for foreign diplomats, leaving very little trust in Peruvian institutions.

Feeling that he had to do something, President Fujimori sent in the troops, who stormed the embassy in April 1997. The raid was largely successful, with fifteen of the terrorists being killed. It was later questioned whether or not some of them may have been summarily executed after surrendering.

At any rate, it seemed that Alberto Fujimori was prepped to seize another term in office as the 2000 election approached. However, Peru's strongman would become so badly embroiled in a drug trafficking scandal that he would finally be forced out of office. Not only that, but he went into a self-imposed exile and relocated to Japan out of fear for his own safety. Yes, just as the 21st century dawned, Peru had found itself once again in a transitional government, holding a special election in the hopes that the people could finally get a leader truly chosen by them.

Chapter 10 – Peru Today – A Precarious State?

"The Report we hand in contains a double outrage: that of massive murder, disappearance and torture; and that of indolence, incompetence and indifference of those who could have stopped this humanitarian catastrophe but didn't."

-Dr. Salomón Lerner Febres

After the ousting of President Alberto Fujimori, new elections were held in April 2001 in which the main contenders were former President Alan Garciá and a political newcomer, Alejandro Toledo. Since so many past elections in Peru had been fraudulent, there were plenty of international observers on hand for this contest. Ultimately, Alejandro Toledo prevailed and was sworn into office on July 28th, 2001.

One of his first major tasks upon taking office was to sort through the mess caused by the war on terror waged by the paramilitary units of the Peruvian Armed Forces. This meant taking a second look at many cases in which Peruvians might have been wrongly accused, as well as holding Peruvian troops accountable that might have transgressed and committed atrocities of their own accord. These efforts would culminate in the Truth and Reconciliation Commission, which submitted its official findings on August 28th, 2003.

Spearheading this effort was Dr. Salomón Lerner Febres, who is said to have taken the testimony of over seventeen thousand people. He also had full access to military documentation of operations waged against

Shining Path and its supporters. Ultimately, Dr. Febres determined that roughly half of all deaths during this conflict could be attributed directly to Shining Path and one-third to other terrorist groups. The remaining third had perished at the hands of the Peruvian military.

These findings understandably generated pushback against the Peruvian Armed Forces and its methods. Even so, it wouldn't be long before their services would be called upon once more. Shining Path soon reared its ugly head and prompted a worried Toledo to suspend some civil liberties as he cracked down on the eastern region of Peru, where Shining Path was wreaking the most havoc. His actions were viewed by many to be ineffective, and Toledo ultimately lost his bid for reelection in 2006, with Alan García returning to the presidency instead.

Garciá just barely won the election, which had gone to a runoff against another opponent, Ollanta Humala Tasso. Ollanta was a former military officer, and he spoke the language of populism in his bid to galvanize the masses to his side. Although many in the electorate considered him too radical in 2006, that would all change by 2011 when Ollanta Humala once again participated in a runoff election and managed to take the prize of the Peruvian presidency.

In this contest, he actually bested none other than Keiko Fujimori, Alberto Fujimori's own daughter. But it certainly wouldn't be smooth sailing for Ollanta. By December, he had declared a state of emergency. The reason? Widespread opposition to mining.

Environmentalists had helped bring Ollanta to power after he promised to curtail mining and safeguard the environment. When Ollanta went back on these promises and ramped up a $4.8 billion gold and copper mining enterprise, some of the very people who had helped bring him to power erupted in fury. Their explosive expressions of outrage forced Ollanta to issue an emergency order to restore the peace. Authorities were given the power to disband any assembled protesters and make arrests on the spot.

This turbulence did not help Ollanta's reelection prospects. And the leftist candidate Ollanta, who had ultimately moved closer toward the center, was defeated in the 2016 election, being bested by Pedro Pablo Kuczynski. As president, Kuczynski made a commitment to help Peru become more inclusive for some of the indigenous tribal groups that had long been on the fringes of Peruvian society.

He directed state-run television stations to broadcast not just in Spanish but also in the native languages of Quechua and Aymara. But as is often the case for Peruvian presidents, he soon ran into quite a bit of turbulence. Most notably, in March of 2018, he was caught up in corruption and bribery charges and ultimately chose to resign. Stepping into the void was his vice president, Martín Vizcarra.

Even though Vizcarra indicated that he was just a stand-in and would not run for office in his own right, he was impeached and removed before his term was up. He was impeached on corruption charges, including allegations that he arranged a $50,000 payment to pop singer Richard Cisneros. Vizcarra was removed from office in November 2020, and an interim president was established, with Manuel Merino being tapped for the job. Incredibly enough, he only lasted for five days before he tendered his resignation. He was dismayed at open protests that had erupted against him and faced an incredibly low approval rating. Merino was succeeded by Francisco Sagasti.

Manuel Merino.
Galería del Ministerio de la Producción, PDM-owner, via Wikimedia Commons;
https://commons.wikimedia.org/wiki/File:Manuel_Merino_de_Lama_(cropped).jpg

In the spring of 2021, Pedro Castillo, a populist politician, galvanized the public to his cause. He toured remote regions of Peru, promising that if he were elected, there would be no more "poor people in a rich country." He also spoke of how he would reform Peruvian industry so that the whole nation would benefit. Pedro Castillo was ultimately pitted against Keiko Fujimori in a runoff before he emerged as the winner and was sworn in as president of Peru on July 28th, 2021.

However, despite Castillo's promises, all he really seemed to bring to the presidency was scandal. He was linked to corruption and organized crime, and in the spring of 2022, he faced impeachment. The efforts failed, but what Pedro did next got him into a whole lot of trouble. Attempting to take a play out of former President Alberto Fujimori's playbook, he attempted to dissolve Congress. In Castillo's case, it didn't work.

Instead, an emergency session of Congress convened, and alarmed congressional representatives once again went through the motions of impeachment. This time around, enough were on board to carry it out. President Pedro Castillo was impeached, and he was replaced by his vice president, Dina Boluarte—Peru's first female president.

But this was not the end of Peru's many problems. In December 2022, massive protests were mounted in the streets. This time, the demonstrators were those who were outraged that former Peruvian President Pedro Castillo had been taken out of office.

Pedro's former Vice President (now President) Dina Boluarte was forced to put Peru back in a state of emergency to bring some sense of stability to a nation that seemed to be teetering on the brink of total anarchy. In January 2023, President Boluarte went on the record to state her desire for a "national truce" so that Peruvians could collectively stop and take a deep breath as they considered what direction they wished to take in the future.

A human rights commission has since released a report that again accuses the Peruvian military of committing some fairly serious human rights violations. Some have even gone as far as to call what happened during the 2022 protests a massacre. It seems that Peru's recent history has involved repeating cycles of bursts of popular outrage on the streets, followed by government crackdowns, and then accusations of overreach by governmental officials.

Peruvian President Dina Boluarte may sincerely hope that everyone can take a deep breath, calm down, and get on with their lives. But as of this writing (May 2023), the situation in Peru remains in a rather precarious state.

Conclusion: Brighter Days Ahead

Peru has certainly come a long way in its history. This piece of land stretching across South America's western Pacific coast has seen empires rise and fall. The Incas referred to the region as the "land of the sun," and they called themselves the "children of the sun." They looked toward the future with the expectation of greatness.

But this has also been the land of Spanish colonizers and a melting pot of several other elements. At sites like the Inca ruins of Machu Picchu, Cuzco, or Vilcabamba, as well as centuries-old Spanish churches, one senses the very real, living history that continues to endure in Peru.

Peru was the land where two cultures collided and ultimately created something new. The descendants of the Incas inherited something much different than their forebearers had expected, but it can still be looked upon with pride. Peru's unique history is just as rich as anything that its gold and silver mines could ever offer.

Even so, Peru has long struggled with its identity in the aftermath of the collision of two colossal civilizations and cultures. And the many reforms, constitutions, and impeached presidents of recent years have demonstrated that Peru is still very much a nation in transition. Peru is a nation in flux, trying to work out its problems and find itself.

So, what does the future hold for Peru? Will all of the demonstrations and protests of the first quarter of the 21st century lead to real change and progress? As of this writing, no one can know for certain. But for the land of the sun, there will most surely be brighter days ahead.

Here's another book by Captivating History that you might like

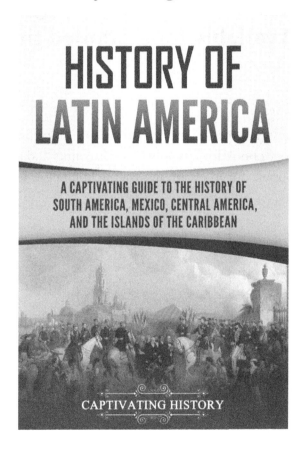

Free Bonus from Captivating History (Available for a Limited time)

Hi History Lovers!

Now you have a chance to join our exclusive history list so you can get your first history ebook for free as well as discounts and a potential to get more history books for free! Simply visit the link below to join.

Captivatinghistory.com/ebook

Also, make sure to follow us on Facebook, Twitter and Youtube by searching for Captivating History.

Appendix A: Further Reading and Reference

MacQuarrie, Kim. *The Last Days of the Incas*. 2007.

Masterson, Daniel. *The History of Peru*. 2009.

Robbins, David. *The History of Peru: A Fascinating Guide*. 2019.

Made in the USA
Las Vegas, NV
02 January 2025